Anyway: The Paradoxical Commandments

1. People are illogical, unreasonable, and self-centered.
   Love them anyway.

2. If you do good, people will accuse you
   of selfish ulterior motives.
   Do good anyway.

3. If you are successful, you will win false
   friends and true enemies.
   Succeed anyway.

4. The good you do today will be forgotten tomorrow.
   Do good anyway.

5. Honesty and frankness make you vulnerable.
   Be honest and frank anyway.

6. The biggest men and women with the
   biggest ideas can be shot down by the smallest
   men and women with the smallest minds.
   Think big anyway.

7. People favor underdogs but follow only top dogs.
   Fight for a few underdogs anyway.

8. What you spend years
   building may be destroyed overnight.
   Build anyway.

9. People really need help but may attack
   you if you do help them.
   Help people anyway.

10. Give the world the best you have and you'll
    get kicked in the teeth.
    Give the world the best you have anyway.

Do It *Anyway*

Do It *Anyway*

*The Handbook for Finding
Personal Meaning and Deep
Happiness in a Crazy World*

Kent M. Keith

INNER
OCEAN

Inner Ocean Publishing, Inc.
P.O. Box 1239
Makawao, Maui, HI 96768-1239

Cover design: Bill Greaves
Interior page design: Bill Greaves
Interior page typography: Madonna Gauding
Copy editor: Kirsten Whatley

Publisher Cataloging-in-Publication Data

Keith, Kent M.
    Do it anyway : the handbook for finding personal meaning and deep happiness in a crazy world / Kent M. Keith. —1st ed. — Makawao, HI : Inner Ocean, 2003.

    p. ; cm.

    ISBN 1-930722-21-4
    1. Conduct of life. 2. Life skills. 3. Altruism. 4. Self-actualization (Psychology) I. Title.

BJ1581.2 .K45 2003
170/.44–dc22   0311 CIP

Printed in Canada by Friesens
Distributed by Publishers Group West

9 8 7 6 5 4 3 2 1

To my parents,

Bruce and Evelyn Keith,

and my mother-in-law,

Misao Tsuruha Carlson

Contents

Introduction

*T*his is a book that I couldn't have written until now. I knew that the Paradoxical Commandments had traveled around the world and had been used by millions of people. But I didn't know *how* people had been using the Paradoxical Commandments.

Since the publication of *Anyway: The Paradoxical Commandments*, I have traveled across the country and talked about the Paradoxical Commandments with people from all walks of life. I have also received messages from thousands of people who have used the Paradoxical Commandments in their daily lives. They have told me how they used the commandments to raise their children, or get through difficult times at work, or set their goals. They have told me that they use them as a checklist, and look at them every morning before they go to work, to help them stay focused on what is most important in their lives.

People have written to me to say that they were experiencing one of the toughest times of their lives, and were beginning to despair, when they found the Paradoxical Commandments on an office wall, or received them in an e-mail from a friend. The Paradoxical Commandments got them going again. I have heard from people who have carried a copy of the Paradoxical Commandments in their wallets or purses for twenty years.

I set out to inspire people, and now they are inspiring me! Their messages describe the personal meaning and deep happiness they have found by living the Paradoxical Commandments and *doing it anyway*.

While I have heard from thousands of people who are successfully living the paradoxical life, I have also met and heard from many people who are having difficulty in finding personal meaning and deep happiness. They are struggling. They are hungry for meaning, but they can't see the potential for meaning that is all around them. They are good, intelligent people. They just can't seem to break out and grasp the meaning and happiness that are waiting for them. They feel trapped.

Trapped in excuses.

Trapped in a difficult past.

Trapped in a difficult present.

It doesn't have to be that way. Each of us can break out of our traps, and find meaning despite the obstacles. What it requires is the courage and commitment to do it anyway. That's what the

Paradoxical Commandments are for: to remind us to *do it anyway*.

This is a practical handbook, a companion to *Anyway: The Paradoxical Commandments*. The first book explained the Paradoxical Commandments. This book is designed to help you use the Paradoxical Commandments in your own life.

Part One is about how you can do it anyway. Yes, the world is crazy, but you can still find personal meaning. You may have a list of excuses, but you can't let those excuses stop you from finding meaning. You may have had a difficult past, but you can leave it behind. Life may be difficult for you right now. It may be difficult because you are locked into "getting ahead." But even while striving to "get ahead," you can find opportunities to "get meaning" as well.

Part Two provides examples of real people—"paradoxical people"—who are living the Paradoxical Commandments and doing it anyway. Their stories illuminate and amplify the meaning of each commandment, and are complemented by questions that you can ask yourself, or use in discussion groups, to reflect on your own life and sources of personal meaning as they relate to each commandment.

Part Three is about how you can make a difference in the world around you. If you live the Paradoxical Commandments, you will become spiritually liberated and personally committed to making the world a better place for all of us. You will be free to be who you are, and you will be actively engaged in making a difference.

Part Four provides answers to the questions I am asked most frequently about the origin of the Paradoxical Commandments, such as what makes the commandments paradoxical, why and when I wrote them, who and what have influenced me the most in my own life, where the Paradoxical Commandments have traveled, and the Mother Teresa connection.

Probably the most important thing I have learned in traveling and talking with people about the Paradoxical Commandments is that great truths are simple, and can be understood by everyone. The truths embodied in the Paradoxical Commandments are fundamental and universal. They are truths I did not invent. I learned them at an early age, and was lucky to find a way to express them that has appealed to many others. I have found great joy in watching others share the Paradoxical Commandments with their families, friends, and colleagues around the world.

Most people can find personal meaning and deep happiness if they choose to do so. The challenge is to choose meaning, and then live in a way that maximizes it. That is what this book is about—living the Paradoxical Commandments and *doing it anyway*. If you live the Paradoxical Commandments, you will find the kind of deep personal happiness that touches your soul. That is the kind of happiness that I wish for you.

1. People are illogical,
unreasonable, and self-centered.
Love them anyway.

2. If you do good, people will accuse you
of selfish ulterior motives.
Do good anyway.

Part One:

&

You Can Do It Anyway

3. If you are successful, you will win false
friends and true enemies.
Succeed anyway.

It's a Crazy World

Okay, you're right. The world is crazy. Your world may be especially crazy. But I promise that you can still find personal meaning and deep happiness.

The Paradoxical Commandments are guidelines for finding meaning in a crazy world. That's why the first phrase in each commandment is about adversity, or difficulty, or disappointment. But each statement about adversity is followed by a positive commandment to *do it anyway*.

The paradox in each case is that even when things are going badly in the world around us, we can still find personal meaning and deep happiness. We can do that by facing the worst in the world with the best in ourselves.

You and I, as individuals, can't control the external world. We can't control the economy or the rate of population growth. We can't control the weather or natural disasters like fires and floods.

We can't control when terrorists may strike or wars may break out. We can't control which companies will acquire which companies, or which jobs will be eliminated, or which jobs will open up. We can work hard, and prepare, and seize opportunities. But there are lots of things in our external world that we just cannot control.

For example, your sector of the economy may take a hit, and the company you work for goes bankrupt. You are talented and good at your work, but suddenly you are out of a job.

You may start your own small business, and a fire destroys your files, records, and product designs. You have to start all over.

You may be in line for a political appointment, but your party loses the election. You don't get the job, even though you worked hard for it and are qualified to do it.

Your supervisor may be very competent and not interested in changing jobs. You are qualified for promotion, but her position is not likely to open up for a long, long time.

There are lots of circumstances that we just can't control. However, there is something very important that we *can* control.

We can control our inner lives. We get to decide who we are going to be and how we are going to live. We can decide to love people, and do good, and succeed, and be honest and frank, and think big, and fight for the underdog, and build, and help people, and give the world our best. We can live our values, and stay close to our families and friends, and do what is right and good and true—no matter what. *No matter what.* The good news is that these are the things that give people the most personal meaning and the deepest happiness.

What do I mean by "personal meaning"? I mean something that is significant and meaningful to you personally. And what is "deep happiness"? I think of it as the kind of happiness that touches your spirit and connects with your soul. People have many names for it. Some people may call it self-actualization. Others call it self-fulfillment. Still others call it being centered. People of faith may call it finding God's will for their lives. But whatever you call it, finding personal meaning is the key to being deeply happy. And that personal meaning can be yours, no matter what.

How am I coping with a crazy world?

1. What do I think is crazy about the world?
2. What is crazy about *my* daily world?
3. What can I do to influence the craziness in the world?

4. What can I do to influence the craziness in my daily world?

5. Do I decide each day to control my inner life? Why? Why not?

6. What is "deep happiness" to me? What words do I use to explain it?

7. How do I feel when I'm not deeply happy?

8. How do I feel when I am deeply happy?

A Personal Declaration of Independence

The Paradoxical Commandments are a personal declaration of independence from all the external factors we can't control. We don't have to depend on the external world for meaning and happiness. We can find them in our inner lives.

Executive coach Ken Hill came across the Paradoxical Commandments in the early nineties. For him:

The Paradoxical Commandments are a reminder that we aren't victims in this world. We are actors who can do what needs to be done—even in the face of resistance. It is interesting to see how some of the leaders and professionals I work with seem to instinctively act in positive ways regardless of the odds against them. But all too often I have clients who are tempted to think of themselves as victims. It is a joy to help these clients strengthen their emotional competencies to the point where they can move beyond feeling victimized to feeling real confidence and a sense of empowerment. One of the questions they have to answer is: What steps can I take, independent of the actions of others, that will get me headed in the right direction? An understanding of the Paradoxical Commandments can help people answer questions like that and can help them go on to build fuller, richer lives for themselves.

Our personal meaning and deep happiness don't depend on the way the world treats us. They depend on how we *respond* to the way the world treats us. How we respond is always up to us. It's our decision. It's about our inner lives, the part of the world that we control.

*Do I understand the factors that I do
and do not control?*

1. What external factors affect me the most right now?
2. How am I responding to those external factors?
3. How can I find the most personal meaning and deep happiness in my response?
4. What can I do to strengthen my inner life, the part of the world that I do control?

No Excuses

The Paradoxical Commandments are also a "no excuses" policy. Sure, some people are illogical, unreasonable, and self-centered. So what? That's no excuse. You need to love them anyway. Why? Because love is an important source of personal meaning. You don't want to miss all that meaning, just because people can be difficult.

Typical Excuses for Not Finding Personal Meaning

Everyone has his or her own favorite excuses for not doing the things that would lead to personal meaning and deep happiness. Here are some typical excuses:

1. *I can't just now. I'm busy. Maybe tomorrow.*
2. *I'll think about it. I'll try to make a plan.*
3. *I'm tired. I just want to sit here on the sofa and watch TV.*
4. *The economy is bad. Maybe when things improve . . .*
5. *The economy is hot. Maybe when things slow down . . .*
6. *I would if I could, but circumstances just aren't right.*
7. *I don't know how to look for personal meaning and deep happiness. I'm not sure how I would adjust if I found it.*
8. *People will think I've gone off the deep end if I do something that is really meaningful.*
9. *People will feel threatened if I do something really meaningful.*
10. *I don't know how to do anything really meaningful.*
11. *I tried it once and it didn't work.*
12. *A friend tried it once and it didn't work.*

And maybe the good you do today will be forgotten tomorrow. So what? That's no excuse. You have to do good anyway. Why? Because doing good will make your life meaningful.

I am always optimistic. I believe that if you follow the Paradoxical Commandments and live the paradoxical life, things will usually work out for you. If you love people, and help people, and do what's right and good and true, you're bound to receive recognition and praise.

But what if things don't work out, or nobody notices your good work? The answer is: So what? You still have to live the paradoxical life. No matter what the world does to you, you have to stay focused on personal meaning and *do it anyway*. Why? Because that is where you will find deep happiness.

In short, if you follow the Paradoxical Commandments, you won't let excuses prevent you from finding personal meaning and deep happiness. You'll do what is meaningful, *anyway*.

What are my excuses for not finding personal meaning?

1. What excuses do I use most often in my daily life? Why?

2. How do I feel when I make those excuses? Why?
3. What are the real reasons I don't do things that give me personal meaning and deep happiness?
4. How can I address those reasons so that I can stop making excuses?

Breaking Away from a Difficult Past

I have met and heard from counselors and therapists who work with people who have difficult pasts. Some of these people grew up in poverty. Some were mistreated when they were children. Some have unresolved conflicts that seem to paralyze them. Some got a "raw deal" from a friend, a spouse, or an employer. Some have been addicted to alcohol or drugs. Some have committed crimes.

What the counselors and therapists have told me is that the Paradoxical Commandments have often been used by people who need to break away from a difficult past. Penny Patton, codirector of the Center for Therapeutic Justice, shares this insight:

The use of paradox in our Correctional Community Recovery "social learning model" offers the participant an immediate opportunity to see another solution or path. It is the perfect intervention for people experiencing a "spiritual emergency" or glimpse of something greater than his or her self. In my work in jails and prisons, the Paradoxical Commandments "fit" because they offer pro-social and specific directives to do something now, in the present moment, that will enhance a cultural or environmental shift that promotes *both* individual and community wellness.

Dave Coleman, a university professor, says:

The power of the Paradoxical Commandments is in the paradox: You can only break away from a difficult past if you acknowledge it. The commandments start with the harsh realities that challenge our everyday commitments to others. But then they go beyond those harsh realities and point to a renewed life, a life that is positive and is not tied to what has happened in the past. They don't forget the truth of brokenness and conflict. They show us a way to heal brokenness and overcome conflict in simple, yet profound ways.

Joe Rice broke away from the harsh realities of his early life. He grew up in a family of migrant workers who picked fruit in orchards in California. His father was a violent man who regularly beat his children, especially when he was drunk. At an early age, Joe witnessed his father kill an African American man for no reason other than his color. In his senior year of high school, Joe hid in the bedroom closet while his father beat his mother. He was too scared to breathe, let alone stand up for her. His father left the house, saying he would be back to get Joe next. Joe found his mother lying on the floor. He held her and cried.

Joe decided to fight. He waited alone in his room with a butcher knife. When his father came back, Joe defended himself, and then he ran. His father's wounds were superficial, and didn't stop him from looking for Joe, well into the night. Joe hid in a vineyard three blocks from his house. He was sent to a secret place away from his family to finish his last two months of high school. Two weeks after graduation, he boarded a Greyhound bus, and set off alone to start a new life in a new world.

What Joe found in that new world was a lot of good people who were willing to help him, and teach him, and encourage him. He decided to become a person who did that for others. After he completed his college degree, he became a Peace Corps volunteer, and then a distinguished educator.

It was clear to Joe at an early age that people are illogical, unreasonable, and self-centered. But Joe dedicated his life to loving them anyway.

We need to acknowledge the past, learn what we can from it, and then move on. If our lives are stuck in the past, we need to get unstuck. It may not be easy. We may need help, and it may take time. But even as we struggle, we need to remember that personal meaning and deep happiness can be ours. We can break away. We can start new lives. We can *do it anyway*.

A Difficult Present

Many of us are struggling with the present. Sometimes, the present is difficult because of the society we live in. But even then, we can find meaning in loving and helping others.

I grew up during the Cold War between the United States and the Soviet Union. The Soviet Union was a communist, totalitarian country, and the Soviets were our biggest enemy. Sadly, while the Cold War was raging, the Soviet people themselves suffered badly. They lived in a police state and they had no freedom. They endured a low standard of living, with little food and clothing, and shabby housing. Their daily lives were a struggle.

In the summer of 1972, when I was twenty-four, I crossed the Soviet Union on my way from England to Japan. I had lived in England for two years as a student, and was on my way to study for two years in Japan. What struck me during my two weeks in the Soviet Union was that so many of the people I saw seemed to be very tired. They seemed listless, as though they were only going through the motions. I saw little spirit, little happiness, little hope. Political repression and economic depression had taken their toll.

And yet, during that trip, I received crucial help from a Russian man I had never seen before and would never see again. I never learned his name. But he saved me from a dire fate because he was willing to *do it anyway*. Without his help, I might well have ended up in a Soviet jail.

Before entering the Soviet Union, I did what all tourists had to do: I went to the Soviet tourism office, known as Intourist, and paid in advance for all my airplane and train tickets, hotel rooms, and meals for the trip. After paying for everything, I set aside some extra spending money to buy souvenirs once I got into the country. I didn't have much—I was on a typical student budget. I had to count my pennies.

Once I got into the Soviet Union, Intourist told me that there had been a mistake, and I hadn't paid enough. The Soviets were greedy for foreign currency, and I became convinced that they would say or do anything to get more of it. At any rate, after a week in Leningrad and a week in Moscow, I had no more foreign currency and only 25 rubles. A ruble sold for about 25 cents on the black market, but the government sold them for $1.25. While I had little money left, I wasn't worried. After all, I had already paid for my transportation, room, and board.

However, when I arrived at the Moscow airport to fly east to Irkutsk, I was told that my luggage exceeded the weight limit, and it would cost 26 rubles (U.S. $32.50) more than I had paid previously. Well, I didn't have 26 rubles, I only had 25, and the plane was departing momentarily. If I didn't make the plane, the rest of my trip would evaporate, because I would miss all my connections and forfeit all the money I had prepaid for my travel and meals. I was particularly angry because the London Intourist office had told me specifically that there was no excess baggage charge.

During the Cold War, there were plenty of stories about Americans being dragged off airplanes or seized in their hotel rooms and never heard from again. I had been told by other travelers that Americans had been locked up and not even allowed a phone call to the American embassy. I didn't know what would happen, but I knew I had only a minute or two to resolve my problem.

I told the people at the counter that I had only 25 rubles. They weren't going to budge. I opened my backpack and began to look for things to throw away to lighten my luggage. I had brought a lot of luggage because I knew it would be several months before my trunk would arrive in Japan.

I started to throw things away. Suddenly, I felt a tap on my shoulder, and I turned around. It was a Russian airline pilot, a young man of perhaps thirty in a blue Aeroflot uniform. He handed me a ruble.

I don't recall him saying anything. I don't think he spoke English. He just handed me the ruble.

I thanked him profusely, hurriedly repacked my luggage, rushed to the counter, and ran out on the tarmac to the plane. I was the last one on board—the plane took off just one minute later. As we lifted off, I thought that I now knew what it was like to meet an angel. He even had those little silver wings on his shoulders!

The Russian pilot had nothing to gain by helping me. There was nothing I could do to help him in return. He knew he would never see me again. Even worse, our governments were "enemies," so helping me might have endangered his career. He had every reason to believe that the KGB, the Soviet secret police, were watching and recording his actions. But he followed a Paradoxical Commandment—and did good, anyway.

No matter how difficult our lives are, right now, we can still love people, help people, and do good. Like the Russian pilot, we can still find personal meaning. The opportunities are all around us.

*What opportunities for personal meaning are right
in front of me, ready for me to grasp?*

My family.
Could I spend more time with my spouse and children?
Do I regularly tell them I love them?
Do I encourage my children with their schoolwork, hobbies, and sports?
Do I make sure my spouse has some quiet time to pursue hobbies and interests or just to relax?
Do I make sure my spouse and I have quality time together on a regular basis?

My relatives.
Do I help my parents?
Do I help my brothers and sisters?
Do I serve as an adult role model for my nieces and nephews?
Am I a friend to my cousins?
If my aunts and uncles had a big impact on me when I was younger, do I tell them—and thank them?

Are any of my relatives old and alone now? Do I visit them—and bring along some of the old photos, so we can reminisce?

My friends.
Am I willing to listen as my friends share their joys and sorrows?
Am I there for my friends during their crises and celebrations?
Do I help out on a regular basis?

My neighbors.
Do I say hello to my neighbors?
Do I invite my neighbors over for dinner or a barbecue?
Do I find quiet ways to help my neighbors?

My colleagues at work.
Do I mentor new employees?
Do I encourage the people I work with every day?
Do I pitch in to get the work done without worrying about getting the credit?

My church, temple, synagogue, or mosque
Do I seek spiritual growth?

Do I join with others in my spiritual search?

My school or university.
Do I give back to the school or university that made a difference in my life?
Do I help others to have the educational opportunities that I had?
Do I donate my time, skills, and/or money?

Nonprofit organizations that helped me and my family.
What organizations helped me or my children grow up—YMCA, YWCA, Boy Scouts, Girl Scouts, Easter Seals, Special Olympics?
How can I help those organizations to help others?

Nonprofit organizations that help those in dire need.
What organizations provide food, clothing, and shelter to people in dire need—Salvation Army, Catholic Charities, my local food bank, a homeless shelter?
Why not call them up, volunteer, collect food and clothing, and raise money?
Why don't I get my friends and neighbors involved?

Associations that promote my values and beliefs.
What associations articulate my values and beliefs—
social, political, economic, religious, or professional?
Why don't I add my voice?

Sometimes, finding personal meaning is difficult for us because conventional pressures seem to lock us into "getting ahead." We get lured into wanting symbols of success like power, wealth, and fame.

We all want to be successful. But the search for success and the search for meaning are not the same. Unfortunately, while we are striving for success, we can miss opportunities for personal meaning that have nothing to do with "success."

Power as a Symbol of Success

Power is a big symbol of success. Many of us think that if we had a lot of power, everything would be better. We could walk around telling people what to do. But what's so great about wielding power? After a while, people will just be unhappy, hostile, and afraid of us. They won't confront us with different ideas, so we won't learn and grow. They will only tell us what they think we want to hear, so it will be hard to find out what we really need to know. And in the end, we really can't order people to do their best. We can only inspire them to do their best.

The first Paradoxical Commandment urges us to love people anyway, and the ninth says that we should help people anyway. We will find more meaning in loving and helping people than in ordering them around. That is why there is more meaning in service than in power. When we love people, and get to know their needs, we can find great joy in meeting those needs. When we are committed to people, they are more likely to share their views with us, stimulating us to grow and to grapple with the truth as others see it. That, in turn, will make it possible for us to inspire them to do and be their best.

Wealth as a Symbol of Success

Wealth is another symbol of success. People really want to be rich. But research and experience tell us that wealthy people are not necessarily happier than others. People who are preoccupied with their wealth often become suspicious and withdraw from daily life, because others are always asking them for money and they don't know who to trust. They build big mansions, but live in only a few rooms. They travel in private jets and limousines, but they don't have many real friends to visit. It is common for them to live lonely lives. Being wealthy is not necessarily meaningful.

People find more meaning in the richness of daily life. What makes a life "rich" is being close to loved ones, having exciting work, and fulfilling one's personal commitments. A rich life is about your daughter's basketball game, viewing a sunset with your spouse, giving your best to a job that is part of an important mission, and pursuing a hobby that stimulates creativity.

What makes life rich is what the Paradoxical Commandments point to—doing good, succeeding, thinking big, fighting for the underdog, building, and giving the world your best. What makes life rich is not money but meaning, and personal meaning is available to all of us in our daily lives.

Fame as a Symbol of Success

Fame is a symbol of success. People want to be famous. They want to have their names in the newspapers and their faces on TV. They want to be mobbed by fans. They think it will be great to be known and adored by millions of people. But there is a price for fame. When you are famous, it is hard to stroll through the mall, or have a quiet meal at a restaurant, or relax at the beach or a park, without being interrupted by people who want your autograph, your attention, or your help. Even worse, you may be stalked or attacked by a sick person. It is harder to feel safe. Finally, fame may not last long. After it is gone, you are a "has-been."

People find more meaning in being known intimately by a

27

few than being known superficially by millions. As the fifth Paradoxical Commandment states, honesty and frankness make you vulnerable. Be honest and frank anyway. Honesty and frankness are fundamental to loving, trusting, intimate relationships.

Having strong, intimate relationships with your family, relatives, and friends will allow you to share your dreams, your ups and downs, with people you love and trust. These relationships are about who you really are, not about who the press says you are. And the relationships don't have to fade, as fame usually does.

Am I a captive of the symbols of success?

1. Do I feel the lure of symbols of success like power, wealth, and fame?
2. Would they give my life more meaning?
3. If I had power, wealth, and fame, what would I do with them?
4. What do I truly feel the need for?

Power, wealth, and fame aren't necessarily bad. However, they're *not enough* if you want to find personal meaning and deep happiness.

That's why the Paradoxical Commandments focus on the things that have given people meaning for thousands of years—loving people, doing good, being honest, giving the world your best.

People can find both success and meaning. Those who seek personal meaning will often receive rewards and recognition, but these are simply a bonus. And those who seek power, wealth, and fame can find personal meaning if they *use* their outward success to help others. Unfortunately, many people who seek success calculate each and every action according to how it will pay off in terms of profit or "getting ahead." The result? They miss the immense meaning that can come from simply doing things that are worth doing in and of themselves.

Your actions don't have to lead to future happiness. Your actions can make you happy *right now*, as you do them. An anonymous act of kindness will not win you a reward. It will *be rewarding*.

What can I do right now?

1. What can I do right now that will make me deeply happy?
2. What can I do right now that will make someone else deeply happy?
3. Why don't I do it?

Yes, it is wise to set goals and plan the steps to achieve them. But your most important goal should be to live a meaningful life. That is what the Paradoxical Commandments are about, and that is something that you can achieve every day. There are some things that you can put off, but meaning is not one of them.

Fran Newman, who has been a vice president of student services and a university professor, tells the story of a friend and colleague who found meaning when he decided to *do it anyway*:

> A dear friend of mine, a president of a large California community college, had a bigger vision of the community

college's role. He made a commitment to improving the college's relationship with the schools and communities of his college district. He became active in civic organizations, served on community boards, and worked with high school superintendents on student issues.

During one of his meetings with the school superintendents, the president learned that a high school within his district was in need of a calculus teacher for gifted high school students. These students were committed to taking the class at 7 A.M. prior to their regular school day.

The president offered the services of the community college math department. The superintendent was extremely pleased the college president would make this unprecedented offer.

The president shared the story of this great community opportunity with the college math department. Instead of a positive response, the math faculty could only give him reasons and excuses why they could not teach the class. The president's idea was shot down.

The college president thanked the math department for their time in listening to his request, and quickly called the superintendent of the high school to say he had obtained a calculus instructor for the gifted high school students. The superintendent was so pleased that he said he'd like to meet the college instructor on the first day of class and introduce the instructor to the high school students.

At 7 A.M. the first day of the class, the superintendent was surprised to see the college president walk into the classroom and greet the students as their new calculus instructor. He explained he was looking forward to teaching the class because he had spent many years teaching calculus before becoming a college president.

Years later the college president said it was the best teaching experience he had ever had. His gifted high school students continue to keep in touch with him today.

The college president had a big idea. He envisioned a world in which the college supported the communities and high schools in his district. He saw an opportunity to act on his big idea, and his faculty shot him down. He continued to think big anyway— and went to teach the class himself.

Teaching an early-morning high school calculus class wasn't in the college president's job description, and it didn't advance his career. It didn't help him "get ahead." But it proved to be the most rewarding teaching experience he had ever had.

Unlike the college president, Magda had to put her career on hold for a while to find meaning. Magda emigrated from Haiti to the United States with her family when she was fifteen. She learned English at a Boston high school, graduating with honors in 1978. She worked hard, earning a bachelor of science degree in occupational therapy from Boston University. After the mandatory nine-month internship at various hospitals and a pediatric center in California, she began work in her profession. By the time she was thirty-five, she had a successful career and a lot of friends. But she felt lonely and unfulfilled. She had a gift for loving others, but had not found a man that she could love and build a family with. Something was missing in her life.

Then Magda's landlady asked her to vacate her apartment, so that she could give it to her son, who was going to attend college locally. This had a catalytic effect on Magda. She decided to take a five-month leave of absence from work in order to travel across the United States, visiting national parks, historic sites, and friends. She also wanted to go to Europe, to see its history, art, and architecture firsthand.

Magda was honest and frank with herself, her parents, and her friends about her career and what she was missing in life. This made her vulnerable to their criticisms. Her parents thought that leaving her job for such a long time was irresponsible. Her friends thought she was too impulsive. During her fourteen years as an occupational therapist, she had never taken more than two or three weeks of vacation. Not only were her family and friends critical, none of them wanted to go with her. She didn't want to travel alone, but she decided to *do it anyway*.

While preparing for her trip, a friend told her that Randy, a man Magda had met seven years earlier, had just earned his MBA. Magda and Randy had been exchanging Christmas cards, and had gone to lunch once a few years earlier. Magda called to congratulate him on his degree and mentioned her upcoming trip. "I don't know what possessed me," she recalls, "but I invited him to join me for part of the trip. He agreed to come along for the first three weeks." When she told her family and friends, they seemed even more upset about the trip.

Magda and Randy began their trip in Seattle. "We were great traveling companions," Magda says. "We had similar interests in nature and the arts. We had no itinerary, and just traveled to the next interesting national park, the next interesting small town, or the next friend. By the time we made it to Louisiana, three weeks later, we had made a commitment to each other." Randy went to a training program for two months and Magda continued her travels. They were married four months after she returned.

"We recently celebrated our sixth anniversary," she says. "The past six years have undoubtedly been the best years of my life. I found a good, loving man, and we have started our family." For Magda, putting her career on hold for a few months made all the difference. "I am still an occupational therapist," she says, "but life is so much more fulfilling and meaningful now."

Magda's honesty and frankness made her vulnerable, but ultimately it led her to a new relationship, and a new life.

John Howell had to change careers completely to find the meaning he was missing. John was a successful sales director at a telecommunications company. He recalls:

My life in sales was grueling. I always exceeded my quotas and made the bosses happy, but after more than twenty years, it was wearing on me. We were constantly restructuring, and firing people, and it just wasn't enjoyable. One day, returning to work after an illness, I began to wonder what it was all for. I started going back to church and doing volunteer work in the community. A friend told me about an opening with a nonprofit group, and with a "leap of faith" I applied for the position.

I was working for one of the biggest companies in the state, earning a good salary. By contrast, the nonprofit organization was near bankruptcy. I was working for one of the top dogs, but I wanted to go and fight for one of the underdogs. I got the job, and within weeks I knew that was where I was supposed to be.

In my sales work, the focus had been on the transaction more than the people. Success was measured in money, not whether you had made a difference or changed a life. Now

I can see how I am helping to change lives—how kids are growing, and getting healthier, and doing things that they couldn't do before. I also get to be a teacher, training a new generation of managers and leaders within our organization. I get tremendous meaning and satisfaction from my work.

Like the college president, you may do something that doesn't obviously contribute to your career to find meaning. Or, like Magda, you may decide to put your career on hold. Or, like John, you may decide to change careers altogether. Or you may simply learn how to find more meaning in the work you have now.

When you see the opportunity to live the Paradoxical Commandments and find personal meaning, just do it. Don't worry about whether it will help you get ahead. Instead, ask yourself if it will make your life more meaningful. If the answer is yes, that is reason enough to do it.

The Fundamental Question

Is it hard to live the Paradoxical Commandments? If you want to find personal meaning and deep happiness, the only thing harder than living the commandments is *not living them*. It is hard to find personal meaning and deep happiness if you are *not* loving people, helping people, and doing what is right and good and true.

Life can be hard for all of us, no matter what we are searching for. So the fundamental question is not: Is life hard or easy? The fundamental question is: Is life *meaningful*? Living the Paradoxical Commandments can make life meaningful for each of us.

If you are already living the Paradoxical Commandments, share them with others. Spread the word. Help others to find personal meaning and deep happiness. Join a growing network of kindred spirits—people all over the world who do it anyway.

If you are trapped in excuses, or a difficult past, or a difficult present, now is the time to break out. The Paradoxical Commandments point the way. Personal meaning and deep happiness are waiting for you.

Don't miss the opportunity for meaning. Don't make excuses. Don't look back. Don't worry about getting ahead.

Do it anyway.

4. The good you do today
will be forgotten tomorrow.
Do good anyway.

Part Two:

❧

Paradoxical People

5. Honesty and frankness make
you vulnerable.
Be honest and frank anyway.

Living the Paradoxical Life

Not everybody knows that personal meaning and deep happiness are awaiting them. I was fortunate. I grew up in a family that lived the values on which the Paradoxical Commandments are built. My parents and aunts and uncles thought that life was about seeking knowledge and wisdom, and doing right by one's fellow human beings. They emphasized hard work, duty, truth, and love. None of them ever thought that their kind of life was unusual. It was just the way people should live. They knew where to find the meaning.

They are not alone. In fact, there are millions of people around the world who live the paradoxical life. They are people like you and me, with jobs and families, joys and sorrows, dilemmas and opportunities. Whatever happens, they love people, and do good, and succeed, and are honest and frank, and think big, and fight for underdogs, and build, and help people, and give the world their best. They live their values, stay close to their families and friends, and do what is right and good and true.

By living that way, they keep their families, organizations, and communities together. They do not think of themselves as heroes or saints. They live the paradoxical life because that is who they are—people who find meaning by doing what is right and good and true *anyway*.

Here are stories of some of these "paradoxical people." Some are the stories of kindred spirits who are willing to share moments from their own journeys. Most are stories from people I have talked with, worked with, and enjoyed community service with—people I admire and respect. Many of them have helped me at different stages in my life, and I am delighted that they are willing to share their stories. I have also added a few stories of my own, as well as some comments on the meaning of each commandment and questions for you or your group to reflect on.

1. People are illogical, unreasonable, and self-centered.
Love them anyway.

I think that the first person I loved who seemed to me to be illogical, unreasonable, and self-centered was my grandfather Edgar Keith. He and Grandma "Queenie" Corinne ran Keith's General Merchandise in a small town in western Nebraska. As late as the 1960s, you could have used the store as part of a movie set in a Western. There were the cabinets with linen goods, the rows of shoe boxes along the wall, and the canned goods on the shelves. There was a hand-cranked adding machine and a huge, golden cash register that must have been manufactured in the nineteenth century. The floors were wooden, and the Calumet clock ticked steadily on the wall. The storefront was so authentic that a magazine for model train hobbyists published a photo of it for readers to copy in building model towns for their train sets.

My parents, my two sisters, and I visited Grandpa and Grandma almost every summer when we kids were growing up. My father was in the Marine Corps, and each time he was transferred, we drove across country, stopping in Nebraska along the way.

Spending a week in a small Nebraska town each summer was quite an eye-opener for city kids. We were impressed with the cows and horses, the corn and wheat fields. We visited a few of the big farms and got to ride on the harvesting equipment. I was especially impressed that everybody knew everything about everybody, going back several generations. I was also amazed that the town didn't have even one streetlight. One summer, my sisters and I all put on overalls and straw hats and took pictures with wheat straw sticking out of our mouths. It was exactly the kind of thing that only city kids would do.

Each time we visited, Grandpa seemed to me to be very reserved, self-absorbed, almost cold. I can't remember him saying more than a few words at a time. I can't remember him laughing or even smiling. He seemed overwhelmed by a solemn sense of duty. That made him very different from Grandma, who was vibrant, warm, and intellectual.

Grandpa kept lists of everything. For example, he put a tag on his electric shaver on which he wrote down the dates that the shaver had been oiled or repaired. The tag dangled as he shaved. When the crows landed in the cherry tree in the backyard, he would pick up his shotgun off the back porch and fire a couple of shells of buckshot at them to scare them away. I always wondered how much of the buckshot landed in the neighbors' yards.

As far as the life of the mind, I don't think Grandpa had had any new ideas for decades. He thought that rural electrification—the process of bringing electricity cooperatives to rural areas—was a communist plot, and he was against it. He didn't seem comfortable with people of other races, but then, he didn't know many. He was very set in his ways, and his ways seemed illogical, unreasonable, and self-centered to me.

But over the years, I began to notice things about Grandpa. He let us kids play with the adding machine and he showed us how to use the cash register. He took us to lunch with him. He let us help out at the store. He showed us his hideaway in the basement of the house, where he had a cot for his afternoon naps. When I was old enough, he took me down into the store basement, which had earthen walls, and let me shoot his .410 shotgun into targets attached to the walls. To him, that was probably my "coming of age" ceremony.

Later, I learned about how he and Grandma had supported their customers—their friends and neighbors—during the depression. They had extended lines of credit to families who no longer had enough money for food and clothes. Most of those lines of credit were never paid. Grandpa and Grandma took the loss.

The summer I set off for college, I took a Greyhound bus across the country, and I stopped in Nebraska. I showed up by myself, wearing a small beard, green corduroy jacket, and sandals. I didn't think of myself as a "hippie," but I am sure I looked like one.

Grandpa didn't say a word. It is true that he didn't parade me around the neighborhood to show me off to everybody, but I knew that he accepted me. That is when I realized that I accepted *him*. We were really different, but it didn't matter. He was my grandpa, and I loved him.

A few years ago, I took my wife and three children to that small town in Nebraska. The store is gone now, but Grandpa and Grandma's house is still there. We parked across the street, and I told my kids what it was like visiting Grandpa and Grandma when I was a kid. We drove out to the cemetery where generations of Keiths are buried. We stood in front of the tombstones of Edgar and Corinne, and laid flowers, and took pictures. I wanted my children to see it. I also wanted to remember how much I loved my grandparents. Grandma was easy to love, and Grandpa was not. But I loved him, *anyway*.

As a parent, I can appreciate the following story, told to me by a woman who is a longtime friend of our family:

"Shut up, you stupid old bitch."

The normal reaction to this outburst would be to do one of these things: slap the person who delivered it; top those insults with worse ones; or, if you happen to be incredibly mature and self-actualized, walk away.

There is yet another option, and it's one that seems completely counterintuitive: hug the insult thrower. This isn't necessarily the most effective or the most sane thing to do in all cases, but it certainly was recently, when my twelve-year-old son daggered me with verbal venom.

In the heat of battle (this time, over delinquent homework and deceptive excuses), I couldn't remember the first part of that first Paradoxical Commandment: *People are illogical, unreasonable, and self-centered.* All I could recall was the second part: *Love them anyway.* And that turned out to be exactly what I needed in order to move my focus from how to get back at my son . . . to how to get him back.

Instead of being blinded by rage—both his and then mine—I could suddenly see with surprising clarity my son's pain, masked up until then by his anger. "Love him anyway," I heard my heart whisper and, in that significant but momentary pause, my arms chose to hug and not hit.

Parents do this all the time: We tolerate behaviors on the part of our children that we would never tolerate in any other relationship. Are we doing a disservice to "love them anyway" when the real world won't? I still don't know what the right answer is in the long run, but I know what the right answer was in the moment. When I hugged the skinny boy/man who hated my guts, he started first to cry and then to sob, surprising us both with his truth.

We stood holding on for who knows how long—long enough for my shirt and shoulder to absorb some of my son's sadness and all of his rage. There were no great miracles that day—his homework didn't disappear and neither did the grounding I imposed as punishment—but something shifted slightly, because I loved him anyway.

We often succumb to stereotypes, and write people off. We don't try to get beyond our first impressions, or our judgment of their faults and foibles, to see the good in them.

Barbara Waugh, author of *The Soul in the Computer: The Story of a Corporate Revolutionary*, was able to see past a stereotype and connect with a colleague. She shares the following story from her work at Hewlett Packard.

Illogical, unreasonable, and self-centered? That was Rolf. A typical nerd. I knew the type, or so I thought. As personnel manager, my job required that I love him anyway—or at least act like it. And acting like it changed everything.

Here's how it started. One day we were planning a team-building event and someone says, "Hey, Barb. Rolf Jaeger is a musician. You should ask him to play."

I groan inwardly. Rolf is a physicist in our R&D lab and I have consigned Rolf to my nerd bucket: very bright, distant, sarcastic, cynical, and unavailable for anything I'll ever think of. I know he'll refuse to play. But it's my job to ask, so I do. True to my expectations, he says no. (People do live down to our expectations, I find.)

I find some other background music for the event, including the segment where we invite our managers to share their personal photos. (One of the company's founders shows his photos of wildflowers, a lifelong passion for him.)

After the event, Rolf comes up to me and says, "You asked me to play for the wrong thing."

"What do you mean?"

"You should have asked me to play for the wildflower collection."

"Oh," I reply. "What kind of music do you do?"

"I'll give you a tape."

I think, Okay, well, whatever, and go on about my business.

A few days later, the tape shows up on my desk. I resent that now I have to listen to it. On the way home, I shove it into the cassette deck. Stunning music fills the car.

I almost drive off the road. The sounds are so mind-bendingly beautiful, I am blown away. One of the songs, "Baby Eric," which Rolf wrote for his son, has me in tears.

I can't see, so I pull off the road.

The next day I call Rolf and tell him his music blows me away. He tells me he plays for spiritual events and, for over a decade, at an annual global healing celebration on New Year's Eve. I end up using Rolf's music at company workshops, for my personal meditation, even as the background music for a major conference.

From then on, anything Rolf is involved in, I want to be involved in: He is landscaping a garden for a homeless shelter, and I go along with other colleagues to help. I discover in Rolf—when I get past the stereotype that's blinded me—an incredibly warm, generous, and loving spirit.

Until I acted like I loved Rolf anyway, I never had a chance to learn what was truly lovable in him, and unlovable in myself—namely, my judgments!

People are illogical, unreasonable, and self-centered. Love them anyway. This Paradoxical Commandment is about the unconditional love that holds our families, friendships, and communities together. I know people who really struggle with this commandment, but it isn't such a struggle if you make two distinctions. First, loving and approving are not the same thing. And second, there are many kinds of love.

None of us is praiseworthy in all things, but all of us want and need to be loved. We want and need to be loved in spite of our faults. We want people to look past our shortcomings and see the good that is inside us. The first Paradoxical Commandment challenges us to do the same for others.

That is what happened to me with my grandfather. I didn't suddenly discover that he was praiseworthy in all things. I gradually got to know him, and understand him, and I began to feel affection for him. I thought his life was too narrow and somber, but I also came to realize that, in his own way, he was doing the best he could. I also noticed when he seemed to be reaching out, in a simple way, to show his affection. I would grin and shake my head at some of the things he would say and do, but his foibles didn't prevent me from loving him.

It is easier to live this first Paradoxical Commandment if you learn how to separate the person from the act. This is an old distinction that parents use with their children: "I love you, but I don't love what you just did." Remember the woman whose son bitterly insulted her? The woman didn't approve of her son's behavior. Not at all. But she still loved him, and when she looked past the insult and shared her love through a hug, her son understood. He knew that she didn't approve of the insult, but she showed him that she loved him anyway. That powerful message changed him, and it became a tearful hug.

I tell my own children that I love them no matter what. Their actions will affect how happy or sad I am, but their actions will not affect my love. It's unconditional.

We know there are many kinds of love—the love between spouses, the love between parents and children, the love between friends. These kinds of love are about strong affection and deep caring. One key to living the first Paradoxical Commandment is the fact that it is also possible to love people we don't know very well. This kind of love, traditionally referred to as *agape*, is an attitude of goodwill toward others. It was this attitude of goodwill that allowed Barbara Waugh to connect with Rolf—to be willing, finally, to listen to his tape and be open to what she heard.

Loving others is one of the deepest sources of meaning in life. If we are not giving and receiving love, we are missing something of immense importance. We can't afford to limit our lives by limiting our love. We need to learn how to love people *anyway*.

Am I living the first Paradoxical Commandment?

1. Have I ever been illogical, unreasonable, or self-centered?
2. Do I know why I behaved that way?
3. Can I love myself anyway?

4. If someone tells me, however gently, that I am being il-logical, or unreasonable, or self-centered, how do I feel? Do I respond positively? Am I defensive? Am I able to admit to myself that they are right, but unable to admit it to them?

5. Do I work or live with people who seem illogical, or un-reasonable, or self-centered? How do I feel about them? How do I react to them?

6. When I come across people who are illogical, unreason-able, or self-centered, can I see beyond their faults and foibles and find something good in them?

7. If I can see beyond their faults and foibles, can I strengthen our relationship based on the good in them?

8. If not, can I love and accept them as they are?

2. If you do good, people will accuse you of selfish ulterior motives. *Do good anyway.*

M.Sgt. Hugh O'Reilly was in Osaka, Japan, with the U.S. Army Wolfhounds after World War II. The devastation of the war was still visible everywhere. One day, O'Reilly went to visit an orphanage located near his unit. When he got there, he discovered that the children did not have adequate food, clothing, shelter, or medicine. He went back to his unit and told the other soldiers what he had seen. He took up a collection. As word got around, not only money but food, clothing, and medicine began to materialize, earmarked for the children. Later, when the Wolfhounds fought in the Korean War, donations were still collected to support the orphanage. They did it by passing a helmet in the foxholes.

For more than fifty years, the Wolfhounds have continued to send money to the orphanage. Every year, soldiers go to Osaka to be with the children for Christmas, and every year, two or three children from the orphanage visit the Wolfhounds at their headquarters in Hawai'i. The orphanage is now government supported and provides good care for the children. But children need more than food, clothing, and shelter—they need love. And the Wolfhounds have been like family members to thousands of children over the years.

Hugh O'Reilly is retired but still actively involved with the Wolfhounds and the orphanage. In light of all the good he has done, I asked him once if anybody had ever accused him of selfish ulterior motives. He paused to reflect. "Yes, a few people accused me of only getting involved because I had an illegitimate child in the orphanage," he said. "They were wrong about that. Actually, they were wrong to think that any of us had an ulterior motive. It was just the right thing to do, so we did it."

The people who accused Hugh O'Reilly of an ulterior motive were probably people who had become cynical and tired, and had given up doing good. People who are just out for themselves often assume that others are too. That seems to soothe their consciences—the idea that they aren't trying to do good, but nobody else is, either. They conclude that other people are just *pretending* to do good, when, in fact, they are out for selfish reasons.

One thing that I found difficult when I worked for the government was that many people operated in the "power model," and they cynically assumed that everyone else was just out to achieve their own selfish ends. So if I proposed something that I thought would be good for my agency or the community at large, others immediately tried to figure out what my selfish ulterior motive was.

I remember meeting with a legislator on a bill that my department had spent a year preparing. We had held workshops for business and community groups, led by a facilitator, to find common ground. We then drafted a bill and circulated it to all the groups for comment, and finally came up with a concept and language that all the groups thought was a positive step forward.

I explained this to the legislator, who listened and then said,

"Okay, okay. What are you *really* trying to achieve with this bill?" I told him we were really trying to achieve what was in the bill. He didn't believe it. "Until you level with me, and tell me what this is *really* all about, I can't support the bill," he said. He made it clear that our meeting was over.

To play his game, I would have had to come up with a harmless, plausible, ulterior motive to explain an idea that was good on its own merits. I was going to be accused of selfish ulterior motives, regardless of whether I had any. So if I didn't have any, I would have had to make some up. If I just went forward on the merits, that particular legislator would be too suspicious of my "hidden agenda" and wouldn't support the bill.

This kind of suspicion exists everywhere—at work, at home, in the community. We are suspicious of people who always try to do good. We call them "goody two-shoes" or "busybodies" or worse. We suspect that they are only doing good to impress the boss, to improve their chances for a promotion, to get publicity or win favor with another person or group. As the years go by, we may come to admit that the people in question are simply good people who enjoy doing good. But we start out by being suspicious.

It shouldn't surprise us, then, that if we set out to do good, we will be accused of selfish ulterior motives. It's just part of the landscape, the culture, the prevalent cynicism in certain organizations.

Such accusations say more about the people who make them than they do about us. We have to continue to do what is right and good and true anyway. The false accusations can't be allowed to stop us. There are too many good things in the world that need doing *anyway*.

Am I living the second Paradoxical Commandment?

1. Have I ever done good, and been accused of selfish ulterior motives? What selfish ulterior motives were people thinking of?
2. Have I ever had selfish ulterior motives?
3. If I was unjustly accused of selfish ulterior motives, how did I feel?
4. What kind of people go around accusing others of selfish ulterior motives?
5. What is life like for people who make accusations like that?
6. If I do good, do I do it noisily or quietly?
7. If I am noisy, does that build resentment and accusations?
8. Do I get a different reaction when I do good quietly?

3. If you are successful, you will win false friends and true enemies. *Succeed anyway.*

Wilson Lau was born in China, the eldest son among six children. His family did not have much money, so when he was fourteen, he had to make a choice. He could become a farmer, or he could leave China. He recalls:

I decided to leave. I wanted to go to Hong Kong, but they were accepting only fifty people per day, so I knew it could take five years to get in. I decided to go to Macao and try to get into Hong Kong from there. It was hard to leave home at fourteen to go somewhere I had never been, without money or friends. I sailed for Macao in June 1962. I met an old lady on the boat who took me to a garment and hat factory, where I worked for the equivalent of one U.S. dollar per week. I guess you would call it a sweat shop. The regular hours were 8:00 A.M. to 8:00 P.M., but I worked until 2:00 A.M. to earn an extra twenty cents per day.

Others noticed that I was a hard worker. I could also

speak a few words in English. That helped me get a job with a box-and-ship company that paid better wages. When I had saved enough money for the boat ride to Hong Kong, I applied for a visa, and was turned down. But eventually I got a visa, and at the age of seventeen, after three years of hard labor, I arrived in Hong Kong. I tracked down a cousin of my father, whose son ran a school. The son needed someone to ring the school bell, fill up the water tank, and clean classrooms. He offered me more money than I had ever earned before. I knew that if I saved the money, went to night school to learn English, and worked hard, there would be opportunities for me.

Wilson did learn English, he did work hard, and opportunities did open up for him in the jewelry business. As the years went by, he became more and more successful. That was when he attracted a false friend:

Another jeweler approached me and said that if I could supply him with merchandise, he would sell it in Canada for a big profit. I was young and eager to do business, so I obtained very valuable merchandise from a supplier and gave it to him. He turned out to be a crook. I lost more than half of the merchandise. Since it wasn't mine to begin with, I had to face my supplier and tell him I had been tricked. I didn't have most of the merchandise, and I didn't have the money to make up the loss. At that point, I could have been ruined. Fortunately, the supplier let me work off my debt.

Sometimes, the false friend is not a crook, but someone who loses control of his own life and torpedoes your success. Jean Varney tells this story:

After working in the corporate world, Roy decided to start a business of his own. It was a small business, but it did quite well. As it continued to grow, Roy found that he needed to hire a general manager to help manage the growth. Through his business associates, he found Tad and hired him to run the day-to-day operations. He liked and trusted Tad. They got along like old friends.

Everything seemed to be going well. The business was thriving. Then one day Roy received a letter. It came to his home, not his office. It was from the IRS. It stated that a large sum in payroll taxes was past due. The IRS was willing to let Roy stay in business if he paid the amount in full. Otherwise, they intended to seize all the company's assets, and all of Roy's personal assets, to cover the amount.

It turned out that Tad had been doing a good job for a

while, but when his wife died, he started drinking. He became an alcoholic, and began to lose his grip on the day-to-day details of the business. He filled out the payroll tax forms, but did not make the tax deposits. He also neglected to file corporation reports. He continued to pay himself, share in the company profits, drive a company car, and enjoy all the perks of his job as general manager. But the business was no longer doing well, and Tad started making up stories to cover himself when Roy pressed him for information.

Roy had become successful, and then a false friend had brought him down. He had worked hard to establish a good reputation for his company, and then he lost the company name because the corporation reports weren't filed. And he had to pay all the taxes that were owed. The company didn't have the assets, so Roy had to take out a substantial second mortgage on his house to cover the costs. It took a while to pay it off, but he did it. Even more important, he moved forward. He reincorporated under a new name, and became a success—again.

Roy never went after Tad for the mess he had made. Instead, he insisted that Tad enter a treatment program and took him to receive counseling. He continued to help Tad in any way that he could. Roy lived the paradoxical life. He not only kept succeeding, he also helped the false friend who had caused him to fail.

Wilson and Roy were successful, and they won false friends. Those false friends brought them major reversals. But they got back on their feet, rebuilt their businesses, and succeeded anyway.

When you are successful, you gain attention and visibility. And when you are *very* successful, others may become interested in your power, or wealth, or fame. You acquire false friends, people who are not interested in you, but in your success. They want to develop a relationship in order to take advantage of you. If you are promoted to a position of prominence, some of your instant friends will not be false friends so much as "positional friends," people who are friends of whoever is in your position. There's nothing wrong with that. You just need to understand that positional friends are not personal friends.

When you are successful, you also make people jealous. There are people who want your success for themselves, or for a friend. They may not know you, but they are out to get you. There are also people who are jealous of anybody who is successful. They attack, in hopes of embarrassing you or bringing you down.

None of this should stop you from being successful. If you are good at what you do and work hard, you will often be rewarded with success. That's the way it should be. Just don't take it personally when others attack you for your success. The people who attack are probably disappointed with their own lives, and you are a handy target. In an important way, the attack isn't about you, it's about them. Stay open-minded, treat your attackers fairly, be patient, and see if some of your "enemies" might end up as allies or even friends.

Above all, stay close to your family and longtime friends— the people who love you for who you are, whether you are successful or not. If you find yourself surrounded by false friends and true enemies, make sure you are taking time to be with your family and your *true* friends. They are committed to you, and will sustain you, no matter what. With their support, you can continue to be successful and find personal meaning.

Am I living the third Paradoxical Commandment?

1. Have I ever been successful and won false friends and true enemies? How did that make me feel?
2. How did I respond to them?

3. Have I ever had positional friends? How did I respond to them?

4. What are some good ways to stay close to my family and true friends when I am surrounded by false friends, positional friends, and enemies?

4. The good you do today will be forgotten tomorrow.
Do good anyway.

Jerry Glashagel helped put together a program that made a difference in the lives of hundreds of thousands of kids and families. He tells this story:

Back in the late seventies, the NBA Players Association approached the YMCA and suggested a partnership. The idea was to have the YMCA bring kids to NBA games to compete in a free-throw contest during halftime. The contests would build up to the play-offs, eliminating hundreds of thousands of kids until there was a single national free-throw champion.

When we were approached by the NBA Players Association, John Ferrell, Bob Phipps, and I were involved in a national values education project. The proposal struck us as the wrong thing to do. It would give the YMCA exposure and provide audiences with halftime entertainment, but it would result in a huge pyramid with only one kid at the top and hundreds of thousands of kids at the bottom. We didn't want to develop programs that would label most kids as losers.

The marketing and public relations people in the YMCA thought we were crazy when we told the NBA that we didn't want to go forward with the halftime free-throw contest. An opportunity for national exposure would be lost!

But we had something better in mind. We told the NBA that we would be delighted to join with them in creating a national Youth Basketball Association in which every kid would play at least half of every game. The amazing thing was that the NBA Players Association agreed!

For a decade, the Youth Basketball Association involved kids all over the country playing basketball. They were coached by volunteer parents, and there were no tournaments or play-offs of any kind. The program began with clinics, proceeded to games, had a mid-season family event where kids played with (and taught) parents, and ended the season with a big family celebration. The NBA players participated in the clinics, family events, and the training of volunteer coaches.

Every kid played. Every kid was a winner! Over the years, hundreds of thousands of kids and their families enjoyed playing and coaching and celebrating basketball.

By 1990, the Youth Basketball Association had faded out. The NBA Players Association had developed different priorities, and there was turnover in the YMCA staff. Attention shifted elsewhere.

The good we did has been forgotten. But it was the right thing to do. I feel great when I think about the positive impact we had on kids and families all across America for more than ten years. It was worth doing. It didn't last, but I'm glad we did it *anyway*.

While serving as the dean of student affairs at a community college, Fran Newman was asked to create and implement a child development center for the college.

The center was long overdue and had become a campus issue and platform for student body presidents. The center would be utilized by the children of the students and staff members of the college.

There was also a secondary need for the center. The early childhood education department, which enrolled an average of six hundred students annually, could use the center as its lab. At the time the students had to go off campus and use the lab of another institution.

For years the administration had tried to encourage the early childhood education department to create a child development center for the college. It seemed a natural since the department would benefit as well as the college. However, the department wouldn't rise to the occasion and considered it an added responsibility it did not want to assume.

My first step was to solicit input from the early childhood department members as I believed it would be a diplomatic gesture and I needed their expertise in making plans. Instead, my visits, inquiries, and attempts to involve them were met with a cold shoulder. They informed me in no uncertain terms that I was the least qualified person on campus to create and implement a child development center for the college.

If their opposition wasn't enough, I found that there was no budget, no staff, no building, and no equipment to fund such a center; initially, it appeared to be a hopeless case. Creativity had to come into play and to utilize the resources of our college community became the challenge.

The students of the college rallied around me with some start-up funds, a retired reading teacher collected toys and instructional materials for the center, and my old college trunk served as one of the storage bins. A neighboring elementary school donated a room for us to begin our services for the evening students. The K–12 district coordinator for child-care services volunteered her expertise to oversee the curriculum and assist with the hiring of teachers to operate the center at night.

Today the college's child development center has moved to a beautiful state-of-the-art building on campus, which accommodates 150 children. It is under the direction of the early childhood education department, which uses it as a lab for the college students. The center is open from early morning to late at night and the college has been commended for having such an outstanding center.

Several years later, a few of the people who remembered that Fran had started the center suggested that she be given a plaque of recognition. Fran learned that the request was denied because the department believed others who were far more qualified had done more since those early days and should be given the credit instead.

"That was fine," Fran says. "I had something that meant more to me than a plaque. I enjoyed walking by the beautiful center and smiling as the children played with their live animals on the playground. What a long way we had come since the days of the borrowed classroom off campus and my college trunk filled with toys! It was enough to just quietly observe that scene. That was all I needed."

When Vernon Wong started his career, he learned that doing good was its own reward. He says:

There is a framed quote in our office by an unknown author that states: "The best measure of a man is to observe how he treats people who can do absolutely nothing for him." I really enjoy this quote because it describes a person who has true character. We all know people who will only do something for another person if they can anticipate some kind of a return. We also know people who will only give you the time of day if you are someone they deem important.

I grew up in a family with six children. My parents had different religious backgrounds. The one thing they agreed on was that each of us should be a good person.

After graduating from college with a degree in business, I considered my career opportunities. My father advised me to do something where I could help other people. He told me that if you find joy in the work that you do, then you will enjoy the satisfaction, and achieve happiness.

Taking Dad's advice, I chose to work as a financial advisor, where I could help people with their financial planning needs and help them to achieve their life goals and dreams. I eventually became the field vice president and managing principal for my region.

I have, with experience, learned that the true reward and satisfaction come in giving of oneself. I remember that as a young manager, my responsibilities included helping new salespersons through training and sitting in on their appointments. In terms of recognition, when they were successful, it was attributed to them. When they were not successful, their lack of success was attributed to me.

I was frustrated by this, and I shared my concern with my manager. He told me that I should not go into management if I wanted to receive a lot of "thank-yous." He suggested that I should only consider going into management if I got satisfaction out of helping someone else develop and become successful. He said that if you enjoy making a difference, then that should be rewarding in itself. Over the years, I have taken that to heart.

This Paradoxical Commandment has helped me tremendously. I have a wonderful relationship with my family, I have done well in my career, and I have many friends. I know that when I do good, it may be forgotten tomorrow, but I enjoy doing good anyway.

For Jerry Glashagel, the Youth Basketball Association was the right thing to do. It fulfilled important values, and it was good for kids and families. It didn't have to last forever. Even if others have forgotten, Jerry remembers, and finds meaning in the memory. For Fran Newman, the child-care center she started filled a critical need. Many have forgotten her role, but she has the personal meaning that comes from seeing the continued success of the child development center. Vernon Wong was confronted with a choice, and decided to do good by helping others succeed, even though he didn't get any credit. He found the personal meaning and didn't need the recognition.

Jerry, Fran, and Vernon all understand that *who you are and how you live are more important than who remembers what you did.*

Do good because that is who you are—a person who does good. Do good because it will help others. Do good because it will always be a source of personal meaning and deep happiness, even if others never know, or those who know forget.

Another way to look at it is this: There will always be at least one person who knows the good you do, and that is *you*. And

71

you're the only one who needs to know. It's your life, not somebody else's. If you know, that's enough.

Am I living the fourth Paradoxical Commandment?

1. Do I do good as a matter of habit? If so, why? If not, why not?

2. Have I ever done good because it will make me look good in the eyes of others? How did I feel when I did that?

3. Have I ever done good, even though nobody else will know? How did I feel when I did that?

4. Have I ever done something good that others have long since forgotten but I remember?

5. Have I ever done something good, forgotten all about it, and then discovered later that others still remember?

6. What difference does it make if people remember or don't remember the good that I do? What difference does it make if *I* remember?

5. Honesty and frankness make you vulnerable.
Be honest and frank anyway.

Dr. Takeshi Yoshihara has served as a U.S. Navy captain, aide to U.S. Senator Spark Matsunaga, a state energy official, and a university professor. But his distinguished career hung in the balance at the very beginning. He had to make a choice. He had to decide how to answer a question that would be critical to his future. He knew that being honest and frank would make him vulnerable.

In August 1945, just a few days before he entered high school as a freshman, Tak's family was released from a detention camp in Idaho where they had spent 3 1/2 years behind barbed wire fencing as a result of the U.S. government's decision to incarcerate and relocate all persons of Japanese ancestry from the West Coast during the war. His father found a job as a dishwasher and rental housing in Renton, Washington. There were eight children in his family.

"My years in high school were uneventful," Tak recalls. The school bus was the only way to get to and from school, which was about ten miles from home. Since the bus left right after school, he was unable to participate in athletics or other extracurricular activities. Classmates were universally friendly but he remained a loner. To compensate, he delved into his studies and spent a great deal of time in the library, where he found solace for his loneliness.

In the fall of his senior year, Tak began to worry seriously about his future. The surest path led to a job as a laborer in a field such as gardening, where so many other Japanese Americans of his generation found employment on the West Coast after World War II.

College seemed out of the question because of the financial condition of his family. But his deepest desire was to obtain a college education. He spent many hours in the library trying to find a way to win a scholarship, and he wrote to a number of universities in the hope of obtaining one.

One day, he learned of an examination being given by a congressman for a competitive appointment to a military academy, which he assumed was West Point. He applied. To his extreme surprise and pleasure, he received a letter from Congressman Thor C. Tollefson shortly after taking the examination, stating that he was nominating Tak to the U.S. Naval Academy. It was the opportunity of a lifetime, and with all expenses paid!

His heart sank, however, when he realized that going to the

Naval Academy meant going to sea. Tak was prone to seasickness. And because of the Academy's emphasis on a record of leadership, athletics, and other extracurricular activities in high school, it seemed impossible to him that he would be accepted. Furthermore, he had bad eyes and had worn glasses since his sophomore year. During this time he spent a lot of time in prayer, and found Bible verses that gave him the courage and the determination to try to enter the school.

Tak passed the examinations. However, the medical questionnaire contained one question that he sweated over a great deal before he answered. The question was whether he was prone to seasickness. He pondered this question for a long time: If he checked "yes," would he automatically be disqualified? His whole career—his whole future—seemed to hinge on his answer. In the end, he checked "yes." He knew that his honesty made him vulnerable, but he decided to be honest *anyway*.

"Somehow, the doctors overlooked my answer," Tak says. He was sworn in as a midshipman, United States Navy.

His first cruise aboard ship was on the battleship USS *Missouri* after his freshman year at the Naval Academy. Mercifully for him, the summer cruise was interrupted because the Korean War broke out, the ship was diverted to the war, and students were released after about three weeks at sea. Those three weeks were long enough to convince him that he had a serious problem with seasickness, even on a ship as massive in size as the *Missouri*.

Tak was not so lucky on his second cruise. After his junior year, he was assigned to a small destroyer escort. Crossing the Atlantic Ocean, he became completely incapacitated. "There is a saying: A seasick person first fears that he will die from illness, and then fears that he will not. I reached that second stage," Tak recalls.

After his return to the Naval Academy, he was brought before a medical board of examiners to determine his fitness for the naval service. The board decided that he should be immediately dismissed from the school.

Crestfallen, Tak appealed the decision, pointing out that in every annual medical questionnaire for the past four years, he had stated that he was prone to seasickness, and that he sincerely desired to continue on to graduation and serve in the navy. The board looked into the matter and decided that because Tak had answered the question honestly, over and over again, he would be permitted to proceed to graduation. However, he would be denied the opportunity of serving as an officer in the United States Navy.

At this point, help came from an unexpected quarter, Commander Joseph K. Taussig, Jr., a third-generation naval officer. Ensign Taussig was the officer of the deck aboard the USS *Nevada* when Japanese planes struck Pearl Harbor on December 7, 1941. Forty-three people were killed and 118 wounded on board the ship that day. Despite having his leg nearly severed by the attack, he directed the gun batteries aboard the ship until he was forcibly evacuated. His heroism earned him the Navy Cross as well as the Purple Heart.

Taussig's leg had to be amputated, and he spent the next two years in rehabilitation. He fought to remain in the navy and won, thereby becoming the first and only "peg leg" officer on active duty. He never returned to sea but was sent to school to become a lawyer. He was teaching military law when Tak entered the Naval Academy. Tak did not know him personally because Taussig only lectured to large classes of students.

Commander Taussig summoned Tak to his office and offered to help if Tak was truly interested in becoming a naval officer. He was the last person Tak expected help from. Here he was, a man who could have become a highly successful naval officer but for the Japanese attack at Pearl Harbor. "I thought that being the only Japanese face in the class might serve to remind Commander Taussig of what had happened to him at Pearl Harbor," says Tak. But true to his word, Taussig energetically went to work, and through his contacts in the navy, successfully intervened on Tak's behalf. Tak became the first American of Japanese ancestry to graduate from the U.S. Naval Academy. He received a commission as an officer in the United States Navy, and served for twenty-one years in positions that did not require sea duty. He retired with the rank of captain. His deep love of education that he gained during his high school years was fulfilled beyond his wildest imagination. He earned a total of five university degrees while in the navy, including a Ph.D. in engineering.

"How different my life would have been if I had not answered a simple question honestly," says Tak.

Years later, Joseph K. Taussig became assistant secretary of the navy. Tak had the privilege of thanking him personally aboard the USS *Arizona*, when Taussig was the principal speaker at an anniversary commemorating the Japanese attack on Pearl Harbor.

In Tak's case, his career was on the line. In other cases, lives are on the line. Here is a story about my uncle, Wally Johnston.

In the fall of 1956, Wally was the aircraft commander of a B-47 crew at Mt. Home Air Force Base in Idaho. General Curtis LeMay, commander of the Strategic Air Command (SAC), had established the Strategic Evaluation Squadron (SES) at Davis-Monthan Air Force Base near Tucson for the purpose of checking the safety and proficiency of the SAC bomber "Lead" crews before designating them as "Select" crews. If Wally's crew successfully completed the week of testing, the crew would be designated a "Select" crew and all three members of the crew would be promoted immediately.

The tests normally took six days. However, Wally's crew was scheduled the week of Labor Day, so they had only five days. The scheduling was tight, and tension was high. The copilot had been experiencing a facial tic for three days.

The first evening on base, the crew had an early dinner and then sat down to plan the next day's mission. The planning session lasted until after midnight. Wally turned in, but by then, his stomach was growling so loudly that he couldn't get to sleep. He knew that food would help him sleep, so he prowled the quarters and the base looking for a vending machine, but he had no luck. He went back to bed, and still couldn't sleep. He remembered being awake at 2:00 A.M.

They had to get up at 4:30 A.M. to get breakfast, "preflight" the aircraft, get a weather briefing, and file a flight plan. Takeoff had to be on the minute. That was part of the evaluation.

The evaluator arrived at the aircraft at about the time the crew completed their preflight inspection. And that's when Wally faced a dilemma. He knew that Air Force regulations required eight hours of "crew rest" in the twelve hours preceding takeoff. He also knew that General LeMay had an SAC regulation requiring pilots to comply with the Air Force regulation. Wally had been in SAC for five years, and he had never heard of anyone aborting a mission due to a lack of crew rest—certainly not an SES mission!

But Wally was severely sleep-deprived. He knew that he could mess up the mission himself or fail to handle an in-flight emergency. Should he do what everyone expected, and go forward with the mission, risking his own life and the lives of his crew? Or should he do what was never done, and abort the mission, risking his reputation and their promotions?

Wally knew that test missions can be rescheduled, but lost lives cannot. He reported to the evaluator that he was aborting the mission because he had not met the crew rest requirement.

The evaluator just looked at him. "We've never had that happen before!" he said.

Wally returned to his quarters, went back to bed, and was asleep in minutes. He was awakened a few hours later and told to report to the psychiatrist. His honesty and frankness had made him vulnerable.

"I knew I wasn't crazy," recalls Wally. "But did *they* know?"

It turned out that the Air Force didn't think Wally was crazy for complying with the crew rest regulation. However, they did want to check him out for fear of flying. Fortunately, the chief test pilot for SES had come from the same bomb squadron as Wally, and he assured them that Wally had no fear of flying. Wally's crew flew home the next day, and the SES mission was rescheduled a few weeks later. The crew passed the evaluation and got their promotions.

Being honest and frank made Tak and Uncle Wally vulnerable, but their careers did not suffer. In another case, being
honest and frank had a different outcome. An attorney tells
this story:

I can remember standing in the courtroom, dismayed at what
the judge was saying. I had moved to collect money owed
to my client, a bank. The statute was clearly in our favor.
But the judge didn't care about the statute. "That may be
what the statute says," I heard him say, "but I don't want to
follow the statute. I want to do what's right." He ruled
against our motion. Instead of winning a summary judgment, we would have to go to trial. The case wasn't over,
but things didn't look good.

I went back to the office and informed the senior partner in our litigation department. The judge's willingness to
ignore the language in the statute could make it hard for the
bank to collect on a lot of loans. By my estimate, the judge's
ruling could affect about $5 million in small loans.

I knew it was my duty to tell the bank. The bank needed
to know. A meeting was arranged, and I met with two of the
senior loan officers. I told them about the case, and what the
judge said. I made it clear that I did not agree with the judge.
He was ignoring the statute. However, if he did it once, he

could do it again. We had a good chance of winning on appeal, but appeals took time and money. In the meantime, I suggested that they look at the loans that could be affected, to get a better sense of the potential exposure. Also, I recommended that we consider revising the language in the loan documents.

What happened a few days later was a shock. The senior partner in my department at the law firm called me into his office and informed me that the bank didn't want me on any of its cases anymore. Since the bank was the largest client of the law firm, and its cases accounted for more than a third of my own caseload as an attorney, my future in the firm was in question.

The senior partner thought that I might prefer to transfer to another department within the firm. However, I knew that wherever I went in the firm, there would be a cloud over my work. The firm's biggest client had asked that I not work on its cases.

I was stunned. Nobody said that I had done a poor job in preparing the brief or arguing the motion in court. Nobody said that I had treated the client poorly. I had just been honest and frank with the client about an unexpected problem that had arisen. That was my duty. That was what it meant to be a professional.

When the bank got upset and called the partner, he was worried about losing the bank as a client. He could have defended me, and told the bank that the judge was off base. He could have reviewed the file and discussed the case with me, and assured the bank that we had done all that we could have done under the circumstances. Instead, to appease the bank, he agreed to remove me from all the bank's cases. The law firm couldn't afford to lose the bank, but it could afford to lose me. I was expendable.

I had no regrets about what I had done. If I had to do it again, I would do the same thing. I couldn't have lived with myself if I had not told the bank what the judge had said. The bank needed to know.

After giving it a lot of thought, I concluded that I no longer had a future in the firm. So a few months after the incident, I resigned. Before leaving the law firm, I visited all the attorneys in the firm to thank them for their friendship. I still have friends at the firm. In fact, that is where I go when I need a lawyer.

The incident occurred more than twenty years ago. From time to time, I see the senior partner who decided that I was expendable. He has long since retired. I bear no grudges. I wish him well. And I am very conscious of the fact that I have had a number of wonderful, meaningful jobs since leaving the law firm. Honesty and frankness made me vulnerable, but it all turned out for the best *anyway*.

Each of these stories is about being honest and vulnerable and risking the consequences. Tak Yoshihara put his career at risk by telling the truth, but in the end, it was precisely his honesty that saved his career. Wally Johnston decided that it was far better to be honest and vulnerable than to risk his own life and the lives of others. He caused others to doubt him, but the doubts were cleared up, and he went on with a successful career. For the attorney, honesty made him vulnerable, and his career was damaged. He paid a price, but he went on to find personal meaning and deep happiness in other jobs.

Honesty is a special quality. When you are honest, people will trust you and will be willing to build a relationship with you. When you are not honest, people will not trust you, and it will be nearly impossible to build relationships. Yes, it is important to be tactful and polite. There is no reason to be rude or brutal in wielding the truth, nor does every truth have to be shared with everyone. There is also a place for confidentiality. But honesty is absolutely essential to building trust and strong relationships.

The vulnerability that comes with honesty and frankness can be good. When you are honest about your thoughts, your hopes, your fears, it is easier for others to get to know you, and for you to learn from them. It is easier to identify new ways of doing things, and new ways to connect with others. Being vulnerable will give you new freedom to grow and find new sources of personal meaning.

Am I living the fifth Paradoxical Commandment?

1. Have I ever been honest and frank, even though it made me vulnerable? What happened? How did I feel about it?
2. Have I ever lied, or avoided telling the truth, because telling the truth would have made me vulnerable? What happened? How did I feel about it?
3. Have I ever had a trusting relationship with somebody who was not honest and frank with me about things that I needed to know?
4. Can I truly know anyone, and build a trusting relationship with him or her, without honesty and frankness?
5. Can I really help people if they aren't honest and frank enough about their needs and hopes for me to know *how* to help them?

6. The biggest men and women with the biggest ideas can be shot down by the smallest men and women with the smallest minds.
Think big anyway.

Ed Kormondy has extensive experience as an administrator in higher education, having served as a university chancellor as well as chair of many accreditation teams. For that reason, he was asked to serve as president of a law school that was struggling to survive. He tells this story:

It was clear that we needed to think big, if we were to get the school on a new, sound footing. So I went looking for some big ideas that would expand our programs and build our enrollments. The first big idea was a court-reporting school. The chief financial officer and I approached a court - reporting school whose owners wanted to sell. This would have complemented the paralegal and law programs, and thus provided the potential for alternative career pathways for students in the different programs. After a preliminary green light from the board of trustees, we did extensive due diligence and prepared a very sound business plan. Then, the board voted down the proposal.

Well, I knew that we needed to think big, anyway. So the dean of the paralegal school and I began discussions with another paralegal school that was about thirty miles away. We thought it would make a good branch campus for us. Again, after a green light from the board, we did due diligence and prepared a very respectable business plan. Again, the board vetoed the proposal.

Ed had been shot down twice, but he wouldn't give up:

Before I left the law school, I got the green light from the board and conducted extensive discussions and planning with another institution to develop a joint MBA-JD program. It would have been a win-win for the students and for both institutions. Unfortunately, my successor let the ball drop.

It was sad, because each of the three proposals that we worked on would have given the law school much-needed financial stability and opportunities for growth. We got shot down by small minds. But you can't let that stop you. You have to think big, anyway.

Ed went on to serve as a consultant for universities in the United States and overseas. He finds meaning in helping institutions solve problems and seize opportunities by thinking big.

Will Hartzell was told that his big idea would never get off the ground. When he was starting his business, Safe Water Systems, there were a host of business advisors, accountants, government officials, prospective customers, and even friends and family who told him that he wouldn't be able to make the company successful. They said he wouldn't be able to find the capital he needed because investors wouldn't risk money on a start-up business that looked like a humanitarian nonprofit organization. They said he didn't have the business training and experience needed to run an international marketing organization. They said it wouldn't be possible to sell the product internationally—it would just be too hard. But Will continued to think big, anyway.

Safe Water Systems was born out of a deep personal commitment to help alleviate one of the world's biggest health crises. Contaminated drinking water kills more than five million people every year. We developed a revolutionary technology, called a solar water pasteurizer, which is a simple, low-cost, long-term solution. Yet the naysayers were plentiful. "You can't succeed," "You won't make it," "It won't work." I heard it all, but I stayed focused on my goals, and my personal commitment remained strong.

One safe-drinking-water project that left an indelible impact on me was in Africa. Our solar water pasteurizers were installed in five locations near Arusha, Tanzania. One site was the Selian Hospital. The hospital was not able to afford a water disinfection system and ran the risk of patients actually contracting diseases while at the hospital.

After our equipment was installed, I was watching the patients as they came to get clean water to drink. One woman was in the hospital because her child was gravely ill. After she filled her water bottle and was headed back to her child, she stopped and looked at me. Our eyes met in one of those time-stopping moments. We didn't speak the same language, but the nurse translated for me. She said, "Thank you. Thank you for giving my child the chance to live."

At that moment I knew that I would do whatever it took to provide safe drinking water for as many people as I could all over the world.

That was in 1997. Since then, Will and his colleagues have installed fourteen hundred solar water pasteurizers in forty-eight countries. The result? An estimated one hundred thousand people no longer suffer illness and risk death because of contaminated drinking water.

The people who kept shooting down Ed Kormondy's ideas were educated people from many different backgrounds. The naysayers who advised Will Hartzell were well-intentioned people, experienced in business, accounting, and government. They were good people, but they were small people, seeing life in small terms. The world needs big people, open to thinking and acting in new ways to solve problems and seize opportunities. The world also needs big ideas, ideas that will really make a difference. A big idea, a dream, a vision of how life could be better, will provide you with a lot of personal meaning. If your big idea is shot down, don't be discouraged. Just pick it up and keep going.

Am I living the sixth Paradoxical Commandment?

1. Do I have a dream or big idea? If not, why not?
2. If I have a dream or big idea, has anybody ever tried to shoot it down? How did I feel?
3. If someone shot down my dream or big idea, what did I do?
4. Why would somebody try to shoot down my dream or big idea?

5. What is life like for people who try to shoot down others' dreams and ideas?

7. People favor underdogs but follow only top dogs.
Fight for a few underdogs anyway.

Sharon Royers tells this story of commitment, doubt, and re-affirmation:

It was a cold, snowy Nebraska morning. Not enough snow to cancel school, but enough to make the commute into Omaha miserable. The daily forty-minute drive was just one of the reasons I was considering a job change. I was tired of the long days, the strain of working in an inner-city school, and the stress of seeing too many children struggling to survive in circumstances that were beyond their control.

Five years before I had made a conscious choice to teach children in an inner-city school. I felt I could reach them. I felt I had something to offer. I felt too few people wanted to work with these less fortunate few.

But after five years of balancing my own family's needs with the work of public education for the less fortunate, I was tired, very tired. I had been thinking about finding a position in the suburban school district where my own children attended school. I rationalized that this way I wouldn't have to rush out the door at 6:45 each morning and would be home sooner in the evening for more family time.

All these thoughts were swirling around in my mind that morning as I drove down Interstate 80 through the snowy muck. I was trying to get to school early because I had a parent meeting scheduled for a second grade student who was struggling with reading.

We had worked especially hard with Jeremy. He wanted to read and he always tried his best. But reading was very difficult for him. We had called the parent meeting to explain what interventions we had been trying and to brainstorm new strategies with Jeremy's parents.

When I finally arrived at school, the young couple was eagerly waiting to speak with me and the small group of teachers. We began to explain all the ways we had tried to help their son. The father listened intently, then he stopped us. Tears welled up in his eyes as he put his hands to his heart and thanked us for all we had done for Jeremy. He told us that he wished he had teachers like us when he was young, teachers who cared enough not to give up. He went on to explain that reading had always been hard for him, too. In fact, he didn't learn to read until he was sixteen years old. He told us that he grew up with an alcoholic mother and teachers who thought of him as a failure. As a result, he landed in prison for a short time. But he now had a family and it was important that what happened to him didn't happen to Jeremy. He promised to read daily with Jeremy, then thanked us one more time before leaving.

After saying good-bye to Jeremy's parents, I sat quietly at my desk, taking in all that had just happened. Then my mind drifted back to words I had read years ago in the Paradoxical Commandments: "Fight for a few underdogs anyway." The swirling turmoil about quitting my job suddenly ceased like the snow outside. Jeremy's father reminded me of what my calling was. So even when I'm tired of the daily traffic, hassles, and stress, I will continue to educate the less fortunate anyway.

Sharon believes that it is only through education that our children in poverty will be free from poverty and all its pitfalls. "I feel fortunate to live in a country that allows me to teach all who enter our doors," she says, "underdogs and top dogs alike!"

Norris Lineweaver remembers what it was like to fight for underdogs during the racial tension of the sixties:

When Arlington College merged with the University of Texas in 1968 to become the University of Texas at Arlington, there was no attempt at first to change the mascot, Johnny Reb. The school flag was a replica design of the Confederate flag, and the school song was "Dixie." Several students wore school insignias of the mascot and applied Confederate decals to their cars. Upholstery on the furniture in the student union center featured imprints taken from old lithographs showing slaves being branded by their owners.

My job at the time was to link local YMCAs and college campuses in the Dallas area, especially with regard to opportunities to involve students in the community to meet human needs. So I wasn't surprised when I received a call in October 1969 from Bob Cunningham, who was the executive director of the Arlington YMCA. Mayor Vandergriff had asked if the YMCA would provide leadership in facilitating conflict resolution involving angry black students and officers of the Arlington Police the following Saturday. He was looking for an organization with the courage to be fair in dealing with racial conflict.

The conflict emanated from a confrontation at a football

game. Leaders of the Collegians for African American Progress advanced on the press box where Mayor Vandergriff was located. They wanted to talk to him about issues in the community and on campus. Arlington police interceded and drew shotguns to protect the Mayor.

While the Arlington Police today is a diverse unit, back then it was an all-white force. I told Bob I would make myself available, but I recommended we find a skilled conflict resolution facilitator who was African American. I had just returned from a rather intense two years in Ethiopia with the YMCA, and I felt determined to ensure that black students were given a fair chance to work through their issues with authorities in the community.

Rad Wilson is a fraternity brother from George Williams College. I called Rad to ask him for his advice and referral. It turned out that Rad had been retained by Admiral Zumwalt, Chief of Naval Operations, to resolve racial conflicts among crew members in the U.S. Navy. I asked him for a favor, and he happened to be available to come to Arlington.

I soon learned that there had been an earlier incident at a football game, during which white students had paraded in front of the black student section, waving the Confederate flag and taunting the students while whistling "Dixie."

After a few passes, black students told them to stop it and move on. White students continued taunting and a fight broke out. By the time the police arrived, black students had the advantage and were seen by police as the ones who had taken the initiative. Police thought the black students had come down from the upper stands and attacked the white students while they were parading on the esplanade.

Rad asked me if I knew students attending the school and what their experience was in class. I said I knew a few who had received scholarships through the YMCA's College Opportunities Program. One student told me that a professor held up his brown paper lunch bag on the first day of class, and said any student darker than his brown paper bag would not pass his class.

YMCA superiors were apprehensive about being involved in the conflict resolution process. Facilitating a dialogue with the black students would make the YMCA itself a target for attack by others. However, YMCA leaders were supportive. They knew that the best way to fight for the black students was to have a facilitated dialogue that could lead to new understanding and less prejudice. The executive director of the Southwest Area Council of YMCAs in Dallas made funds available to support the conflict resolution dialogue.

Nine Arlington Police officers showed up early Saturday morning, along with twelve black students and a few white students. Rad facilitated the confrontation dialogue for nine hours. The truth came out. Tensions were relieved.

What then happened was remarkable. The nine officers met with the chief of police and requested that this dialogue continue as part of their annual training. The police chief called Mayor Vandergriff to report the positive experience. The mayor came to the YMCA executive director's home that Saturday evening to meet with Rad Wilson and me. That evening, from home, he called the chancellor of the University of Texas.

The following Monday, the president of the University of Texas at Arlington announced that the school no longer had a mascot, flag, or school song. The furniture with inappropriate designs was removed from the student center. Later, the college president announced the appointment of a task force to develop and propose a new mascot, flag, and song to be introduced in two years. Today, students at the University of Texas at Arlington are known as the Mavericks, with a different flag and song. Few remember what the mascot, flag, and song used to be.

What happened to the so-called black militants, as they were initially labeled in the local newspaper accounts? Some were hired by the YMCA to serve as camp counselors the following summer, to lead positive programs for children. The programs were widely acclaimed by parents. The students later graduated from the college, and went on to lead responsible lives.

It was a tense situation, but YMCA leaders took a risk and facilitated a successful resolution. "It taught me that underdogs can be top dogs—when the truth sets them free," says Norris.

Fighting for underdogs in higher education is a passion of Dr. Linda Serra Hagedorn.

A somewhat large community college is located only blocks away from the large urban university where I'm employed. Whereas the students at my university are predominantly white, the community college is almost entirely composed of Hispanic and African American students. While the university has beautifully manicured lawns and flowerbeds, the neighboring community college is a crammed set of buildings resting on concrete, where almost every square inch of space is occupied. But most importantly, a comparison of the socioeconomic status levels of the students at the two institutions reveals the strongest contrast of all. For the most part, the university serves the upper middle and upper classes, while the community college serves the poor and working classes. By all accounts, community colleges are the underdogs of the postsecondary arena.

Two years ago I made a plea to increase the dialogue, and subsequently the transfer rate, between my university and its neighboring community college. Indeed, it looked like I might even be successful as I managed to bring a very high level administrator to speak to the community college president. But my hopes soon vanished as the meeting progressed and it became clear that the administrator's self-perceived purpose was to inform the community college of the wonderful work it was doing. When the community college representative and I brought up the topic of increasing the rate of transfer, the university administrator responded, "the university isn't interested in increasing the rate of transfer. We believe that it is in the best interest of the student to start the university as a freshman and to continue through graduation."

The university administrator's words ignored the truth that most underdogs who go to college begin at community colleges. The university spoke loudly about diversity and a welcome of low-income students, yet it wasn't willing to open its door to the biggest flow of students fitting that description.

Dr. Hagedorn was disappointed, but she continues to fight for underdogs anyway.

Underdogs are, by definition, at a disadvantage. They do not have as much power, or wealth, or fame, or experience, or health as others. Millions of people in this country are born to lives of poverty, and racism, and limited access to education and health care. They didn't ask to be born to these disadvantages, but they were. Sharon Royers, Norris Lineweaver, and Linda Serra Hagedorn have found personal meaning by fighting for underdogs. It's not easy, but they fight for them, anyway.

Some underdogs are people with good ideas that have not yet been accepted. Other underdogs are simply new to their organizations or communities, and challenge those in power, wanting to bring about change. The fact is that most new ideas begin with one person or a small group of people. These people are usually underdogs when they first voice their ideas. But if we help them, and stand with them, and join our voices with theirs, change is possible. The new idea can become an accepted reality.

But there is a risk—the risk of failure and disapproval. We could find ourselves suddenly becoming underdogs, too. So we like to cheer for underdogs, but we are reluctant to put our own families, or careers, or reputations on the line to support them. Even when our hearts are with the underdog, we tend to follow the top dogs. It's the safe thing to do.

Of course, not every underdog is right, but when you see one who is, think about the kind of help you can give. It could turn out to be one of the most meaningful things that you ever did.

Am I living the seventh Paradoxical Commandment?

1. Have I ever been an underdog? How did it make me feel?
2. Do I know any underdogs? Do they have a good cause? Can I help them?
3. What risks do I take if I help an underdog? Are the risks worth it?
4. What are the benefits of fighting for an underdog?

8. What you spend years building may be destroyed overnight. *Build anyway.*

Les Miyamoto tells this story about his father, Sadao, who worked on the Dole Pineapple plantation on the island of Lana'i:

> His nickname was "Franchot." He would stay up till the wee hours of the morning reading Zane Grey novels, then go to work on the plantation as a fledgling surveyor. He would drag himself out of bed and go to work, dreaming of being an engineer, building bridges and dams all over the world. Building a bridge in the South American jungle was a frequent thought.
>
> He was just twelve years old when his dad suddenly died. Their family had just moved to work on the plantation. Franchot's mother supported them by working at one of the boarding houses on the plantation. His eighth-grade teacher deemed Franchot unworthy of further education, so he started working in the fields as a "mule boy" at the age of thirteen.

He worked at a number of jobs, finally ending up in a crew that worked on infrastructure like roads and irrigation projects all over the plantation. Eventually he became a surveyor, went to night school, and received his high school diploma when he was in his forties. He stayed on the plantation, and it provided the means for him and his wife, Susan, to raise a family of five children.

Franchot and his crew surveyed and designed fields according to tried-and-true farming principles and to accommodate mechanized farming. To them, the fields were beautiful living sculptures. As the years passed, the plantation no longer used mules to plow and till the fields; they used tractors. Crops were still planted by hand, but irrigation and harvesting were done using heavy trucks and specially designed harvesting rigs. Franchot and his crew even designed dams as part of an overall drainage system for the plantation.

Then the plantation owners decided to expand their operations in Honduras and Thailand. They needed someone to help the workers there understand the nuances of preparing the land for growing pineapples. So forty years after reading those Zane Grey novels, Franchot fulfilled his dream of working overseas, leaving the island of Lana'i in the Hawaiian Islands for temporary duty in Honduras in 1973 and

Thailand in 1974. He wasn't building bridges, but years of working in surveying, planting, and field preparation gave him the practical knowledge necessary to help the folks at Dole Pineapple's new plantations in Honduras and Thailand.

When Franchot retired, he had worked for forty-nine years and six months. He had spent his life working, learning, and helping to build the plantation, first as a mule boy, then on to design and field preparation. Unfortunately, by the early nineties it was no longer feasible for Dole to continue operating its Lana'i plantation. The fields he and his crew had painstakingly laid out became fallow, overgrown by grass and weeds. Vague outlines were all that remained of the once beautifully sculpted landscape. What he had spent years building was gone.

It saddened Franchot to see the plantation close down and the fields go fallow, but he knew that it didn't take away from all that he had accomplished in life. He had built fields, roads, and dams. More important, he had managed to meet life's challenges, losing his father when he was twelve, starting work full-time at the age of thirteen, becoming a surveyor, earning his high school diploma in night school, and working steadily for nearly fifty years.

Franchot could have bemoaned the passing of the "good

old plantation days" and the fields that he had worked so hard to design, but he didn't. When he reminisced, he talked about how fortunate he was to have lived life as he did.

"He lived his life according to the Paradoxical Commandments," Les says. "He didn't have a name for them, but he lived them."

In the late seventies, I became passionate about renewable energy, and I have spent many years supporting its development. While our coal and oil resources will one day be depleted, renewable energy resources can continue indefinitely. They are based on a simple fact: Every day, our planet receives new energy from the sun. That energy can be extracted from solar, wind, hydro, ocean thermal, and biomass resources.

I worked in the Hawai'i State Department of Planning and Economic Development. Hawai'i has no oil or coal resources, and depends on imported oil for nearly 90 percent of its energy. However, the islands are rich in renewable energy. Shifting to renewable energy would have a major, positive impact on jobs, the economy, and the environment in Hawai'i.

One of my favorite technologies has always been ocean thermal energy conversion, or OTEC. An OTEC plant uses the temperature difference between deep, cold ocean water and warm, surface water to drive a heat engine. The worldwide potential for OTEC is huge, and the technology can be adapted to local conditions. OTEC plants can be located onshore, on towers located offshore, or on floating structures like barges.

Because the temperature differential is available both day and night, year-round, OTEC power is reliable. OTEC plants do not pollute the air. The deep, cold ocean water that is brought up during the process is rich in nutrients and can be used for aquaculture—to raise shellfish, shrimp, lobster, or seaweed. Open-cycle OTEC systems can produce drinking water.

The State of Hawai'i began its commitment to OTEC in 1974, with the establishment of a natural energy institute at the University of Hawai'i and a 320-acre laboratory on the island of Hawai'i, where the Seacoast Test Facility was later located. On August 2, 1979, Mini-OTEC, located offshore Hawai'i, became the first at-sea, closed-cycle OTEC plant to produce net energy. The federal government launched its test project, OTEC-1, in 1980 onboard the SS *Ocean Energy Converter*, which floated off the coast of the island of Hawai'i and tested heat exchangers. With hard work and planning, Hawai'i became the national center for OTEC research and demonstration.

The federal Department of Energy was committed to funding research and the first major pilot plant. The understanding was that after that pilot plant was tested, the private sector would assume the lead and make major investments in OTEC as an ongoing commercial enterprise. In 1980, the federal government issued a notice that it would fund the design and construction of a 40-mcgawatt OTEC pilot plant. The plant was expected to cost $280 million.

We were ready. A year earlier, we had formed a committee to coordinate our bid for the plant. The electric utility company, a local construction firm, the University of Hawai'i, and the state government worked together generating and collecting data. The state legislature, governor, and congressional delegation all supported the effort. I was involved in the interaction with the companies that were considering Hawai'i as a site. Nine proposals were submitted by private firms, and three of them—General Electric, TRW, and Lockheed—bid Hawai'i as the site for their proposals.

After years of work, we were on the verge of a major breakthrough in renewable energy—an OTEC pilot plant big enough to really prove the technology on a commercial scale. Then the political tide turned. President Reagan was elected in 1980, and by 1981, he had announced that he wanted to eliminate the Department of Energy and the OTEC program. The federal funding dried up, and the 40-megawatt plant was dropped. The private companies, which had already invested millions of dollars on development, were not willing to move forward with a plant on their own. It was just too risky for a single firm.

It was over. What we had spent years building was gone, almost overnight.

While I deeply wish that the pilot plant had been built, I have no regrets about the thousands of hours I spent on OTEC development. We owed it to ourselves and the people of our state to give the opportunity our best efforts. For me personally, OTEC development was meaningful work, a source of real joy. I am proud of what we did, and I would do it again. In fact, when I read about the amount of oil our nation imports, and the political problems that stem from our dependence on foreign oil, I know that we *need* to do it again! We need to keep building *anyway*.

One man who lost what he spent years building is Wally Amos, known as "Famous Amos," the chocolate chip cookie entrepreneur. Wally is a warm, enthusiastic, irrepressible spirit who has inspired millions during his lifetime.

Wally became the father of the gourmet cookie industry when he opened his Famous Amos Chocolate Chip Cookie Company in a small store on Sunset Boulevard in Los Angeles in 1975. He made use of his experience as a talent agent with the William Morris Agency to make his cookies fashionable in Hollywood. Then his cookies became a supermarket basic, as they spread throughout the country.

Business boomed, and the company grew rapidly. Within five years, Wally's face, his trademark battered Panama hat, his embroidered Indian pullover shirt, and his grin had become known throughout America. "Here was proof that a black high school dropout from a broken home in Harlem could still make it in this country," Wally recalls.

But as the years went by, Wally was finding it harder to manage the business. The company started losing money, so he brought in outside investors, who gradually took a larger and larger percentage of the ownership of the company.

By 1985, Wally had lost ownership completely. He became an employee, under contract to promote and publicize the company. He couldn't become involved in any other commercial activities without the company's consent. He also had to sign a "non-compete" clause, preventing him from being involved with any other company that might produce or market cookies for two years after he ceased to be an employee.

The company that Wally had created continued to change hands. Finally, the day came when the new management wanted Wally out. He was terminated in 1989. He no longer had any formal ties to the company he had created. "I left the company I founded, and I left with nothing," Wally says.

Wally came to accept what had happened. "I reminded myself that life is a process, and everything in it works together for the best," he said. "I knew I was not a victim."

Wally began a career as a lecturer, and he continued his

charitable work as national spokesman for Literacy Volunteers of America, as well as serving on the boards of Cities in Schools, the Napoleon Hill Foundation, the Aloha United Way, and the YMCA of Honolulu. Wally was honored with the Horatio Alger Award, the President's Award for Entrepreneurial Excellence, and the National Literacy Honors Award.

When the two years in the "non-compete" clause were over in 1991, Wally got back to business. But when he set out to launch two dolls, Chip and Cookie, his former company sued him to stop him from using his name or likeness in promoting his new products. Wally was broke, and turned to his friends to raise the money for his legal defense. His friends supported him, but the judge ruled against him. He had lost the right to use his own name and face in developing any new products on his own.

"I was stunned," says Wally. "But then I realized that I didn't exist for my name, I existed for my spirit. Everything else was an accessory."

There was a name he couldn't use, but there were millions more to choose from. He decided to be Uncle Noname (pronounced *no-NAH-may*), and began producing and selling chocolate chip cookies again. A year later, he regained the right to use his name, likeness, and reputation to market his new cookies. His old company still owned "Wally Amos" as a trademark for food products, but Wally could use his name as a trademark for nonfood merchandise like Chip and Cookie dolls.

In the decade since then, Wally Amos has built a new life as a speaker, author, and entrepreneur. His new businesses include Uncle Wally's Muffins, Aunt Della's Cookies, Wally Amos Presents Chip & Cookie (a concept developed around two chocolate chip cookie dolls), watermelon apparel, and inspirational books and tapes. His most recent book is *The Cookie Never Crumbles: Inspirational Recipes for Everyday Living.*

"I am better off now than when I started," Wally says. "My life got better, and I got stronger. Life is never what it seems. It is always more!"

Franchot spent nearly fifty years building a pineapple plantation, and then saw it close down. But he knew that he had accomplished a lot, anyway. He talked about how fortunate he had been to live the life that he lived. I spent a few years working with others on an OTEC pilot plant program, and saw the program shut down, almost overnight. But I am proud of what my colleagues and I accomplished, supporting the development of a technology that may still make a major contribution to the world. Wally Amos built an empire, lost an empire, and then built a new life *anyway*.

Organizations, relationships, physical objects—all the things that you build may be destroyed during your lifetime. You could lose them overnight. If they survive your own passing, they may not survive for long, because the world will continue to change. Buildings will be torn down, new inventions will replace the old, new ideas will be adopted, new organizations will arise, new relationships will be formed.

But it is worth building anyway. It is worth it because the act of building brings joy and satisfaction. And even when the things you build are destroyed, that doesn't change what you accomplished. What you accomplished was real. You will always be able to look back on it with pride and pleasure. What you accomplished can be a source of meaning forever.

Am I living the eighth Paradoxical Commandment?

1. Have I ever lost something that I spent years building? How did it feel?
2. What caused the loss? Did I know it could happen?
3. What can I learn from the loss?
4. What are the reasons for building again? What would I do differently this time?

9. People really need help but may attack you if you do help them. *Help people anyway.*

I worked for a land development company for several years. One of the company's properties was a popular tourist attraction. Right next door was a nonprofit organization that provided employment for the handicapped. The company wanted to be a good neighbor, so it leased parking space to the nonprofit for $1 per year, allowed the nonprofit to put up a large sign to advertise its shops and restaurant, and even put up ads for the nonprofit in the company's own facilities. I was proud of the company's generosity toward its neighbor.

Years later, the company applied for a zoning variance to expand its facility and add a restaurant so that it could attract more tourists. The nonprofit organization was very likely to benefit by the increase in tourism, but it was worried that its own restaurant business would suffer, so it publicly attacked the company and opposed the zoning change.

The company could have played hardball and fought back. It could have literally "pulled the plug" on the nonprofit organization. But it didn't. I am proud to say it quietly withstood the attack and continued to help the nonprofit *anyway*. Today, the company and the nonprofit have a very close, supportive relationship.

A friend of mine who is a pastor says that he is a helper because so many people have helped him along the way. He has been encouraged, confronted, and challenged by people who cared and never gave up on him, and he tries to do the same for others. He told me this story:

I remember an incident several years ago with a friend who I'll call Bill. He had been on medication since his teens and was fairly stable, living with his family, able to hold down a job. We met on a regular basis for a snack and to just visit. One day I got a call from one of his family members. He had gone off his medication for a couple of days, and was on a rampage in the house. I came quickly and discovered him pacing wildly in the living room. "Bill, I'm here to help," I said. "It's going to be all right!" His response was a vicious "Get away from me—I don't want your help. I hate you!" He pushed his mother to the ground, threw furniture around, and ran out of the house. His family and I stood there helpless, wondering what to do next.

The police found him wandering in a shopping center

and brought him to a mental health facility in a nearby city. I was able to visit him several times and reestablish our relationship. He regained his stability, and now, years later, he continues with a balanced life, working regularly, still at home with a loving family. Shortly after the traumatic incident, he said to me, "Thank you for sticking with me and not giving up on me. You are a true friend."

Parents know what it's like to be screamed at by children who don't appreciate their help, only to have them come back later to say, "Thanks, Dad. Thanks, Mom. You never gave up on me. Thanks for caring." That's the key— to keep on caring. Never give up on anyone, even if they attack you when you try to help them.

John Welshons is a teacher, lecturer, and author of *Awakening from Grief*. He shares the story of his relationship with his father, and what he learned during their final day together.

It is astounding how often we will attack the very people most capable of helping us—sometimes the very people we love the most. It is especially true for those who work with parents as they are aging and dying.

My dad and I had had an extremely tumultuous relationship when I was growing up. Later, as his health deteriorated, he became increasingly cantankerous, irrationally nasty, and volatile. His behavior began to mimic the way he had behaved in earlier years when he was drunk. Sometimes, he was warm and kind. Then suddenly, without warning, he would lash out in a rage, abusing everyone around him, including those most intimately connected with caring for him.

On the day before he died, I stood at his bedside and he railed at me in an unrelenting, abusive diatribe about what a disappointment I was to him and what a failure I had been as a son. I looked into my own heart and realized that after all those years, after all the emotional ups and downs in our relationship, I just felt compassion for his predicament. I realized I had given him everything I could in the way of time, energy, support, and love. I just felt sad that he was so caught in his own mind he couldn't recognize it.

Finding no sense of anger or reactivity in myself, and no place where his accusations inspired guilt, I just looked deeply into his eyes and in the middle of his diatribe quietly spoke from the depths of my heart.

"I love you, too, Dad." And I *really* meant it.

And the most amazing thing happened. When I said that, his entire body relaxed. His head melted back into the pillow. His body settled into the bed. The muscles of his face softened. A sweet, peaceful smile spread from his lips to his cheeks and continued getting bigger and broader. His eyes gazed up toward the heavens and he raised his right arm up off the bed. He moved slowly and deliberately. Eventually his right hand softly touched my shoulder, and he sweetly rested his palm there. I could feel his fingers gently squeezing my shoulder with affection. He lifted his hand and patted my shoulder, subtly communicating deep love and admiration.

He spoke softly and slowly, in scarcely more than a whisper: "Good . . . Good . . . Good," he kept saying, as he smiled toward heaven and patted my shoulder.

And what I felt at that moment was quite remarkable. I felt like he was relaxing, and saying to himself, "Thank God. After thirty-three years the kid finally got it. He *finally* realizes that it isn't about *me*, it's about *him*. *Finally* I can die in peace."

Finally I had come to know that whether or not I loved him wasn't contingent on his behavior. It was totally up to me.

He died the next day. And I recognized that one of the greatest teachings he ever gave me was the gift of learning to love and help just because it's the right thing to do, not because we want something in return. After all, love just *feels* good.

He also showed me that when people are nasty and unpleasant, it's really because they, themselves, are in pain. And he taught me that the greatest joy comes when—even though people attack us—we love and help them *anyway*.

The land development company was attacked by the nonprofit organization, but it continued to help, anyway. That made it possible for the company to build a very close relationship with the nonprofit organization in later years. The pastor continued to help Bill even after Bill attacked him. When Bill recovered, he thanked the pastor for being a true friend. John Welshons withstood the abusive diatribe of his father, and was able to tell his father he loved him. Those words gave his father peace the day before he died.

Some people are reluctant to ask for help or resent the fact that they need it. Being assisted by others makes them feel dependent or ignorant. And so, when someone tries to help them, they attack. Be thoughtful and attentive. Do your best to understand exactly what they need, and to preserve their dignity. Help them to grow and become self-reliant to the extent that they are willing and able. Of course, they may still attack you, but don't let that stop you— you will still find a lot of personal meaning by helping them.

Am I living the ninth Paradoxical Commandment?

1. Have I ever been attacked by people I helped? How did that make me feel?

2. If others attacked me for helping them, did they explain what they think I did wrong? Is it likely that there were deeper reasons for the attack that they did not share?

3. What did I learn? Would I do things differently next time?

4. How do I feel when others help *me*?

5. Have I ever attacked others who helped me? If so, why?

10. Give the world the best you have and you'll get kicked in the teeth.
Give the world the best you have anyway.

If ever there was a group of people who lived the tenth Paradoxical Commandment, it was the 442nd Regimental Combat Team in World War II. The 442nd consisted entirely of Americans of Japanese ancestry.

When Pearl Harbor was attacked on December 7, 1941, there were hundreds of thousands of Americans of Japanese ancestry living in Hawai'i and on the U.S. mainland. Immediately after the attack, the FBI began arresting them. The U.S. military began discharging and reassigning them; those on the mainland were segregated out of their units. Less than two months later, Japanese Americans were barred from all civil service positions. In February 1942, President Roosevelt signed Executive Order 9066, which set the stage for the incarceration of 120,000 Japanese Americans in detention camps on the mainland. Japanese Americans lost their homes, their jobs, and their freedom. Although there was no proof that they had been disloyal in any way, Japanese American men, women, and children were forced into detention camps, where they spent years behind barbed wire as prisoners of their own country.

If ever a group of people had reason to be bitter about their country, it was Japanese Americans at the beginning of World War II. They had given America their best and had been kicked in the teeth. What happened next was extraordinary. Thousands of young Japanese American men came forward to give their country the best they had *anyway*.

After Pearl Harbor was bombed, the University of Hawai'i ROTC unit, with 370 students, was dismissed as a unit. The young men reacted by forming a labor force they called the Varsity Victory Volunteers, offering to assist the war effort in any way that they could. Meanwhile, the Hawai'i National Guard segregated Japanese American guardsmen into the 100th Infantry Battalion and sent them to Wisconsin for training.

Because of the exemplary conduct of the Varsity Victory Volunteers and the 100th Battalion, the army agreed to form an all–Japanese American regiment. The plan called for 1,500 volunteers from Hawai'i and 3,000 from the mainland. When the call went out in Hawai'i, 10,000 young Japanese Americans volunteered, and 2,900 were accepted.

By September 1943, the 100th Infantry Battalion had landed at Salerno, Italy, and began offensive attacks against the Germans. More than a year later, after intensive training, the 442nd joined them northwest of Rome, and the two units became known as the 442nd Regimental Combat Team—the "Go for Broke" regiment.

The 442nd may be best known for its rescue of the "Lost Battalion" in October 1944. The Lost Battalion was a Texas battalion of 275 men of the 141st Regiment, 36th Division. The battalion had been surrounded by the Germans for almost a week, and they were running low on food and ammunition. Their comrades in the 141st Regiment couldn't reach them. The 442nd was ordered to rescue them at any cost.

They knew why they were chosen for the mission—the army thought they were expendable. But they welcomed the opportunity to prove their commitment.

The fighting took place in the snow, frost, rain, dense foliage, and darkness of the French Vosges Mountains. Sometimes, they couldn't see more than a few feet in front of them because of the fog. They fought from tree to tree, against hidden machine gun nests and infantry with tank support. They faced mortar and artillery fire and had to cross minefields and booby traps. After four days of intense fighting, the 442nd succeeded in rescuing the 217 remaining Texans.

The 442nd suffered 814 casualties—more than 200 dead and 600 wounded. Company I, which began the battle with 100 men, had only 8 riflemen and 1 sergeant left. Company K, which began with 150 men, had only 17 riflemen and 1 sergeant left. Both companies had lost all their officers. The 442nd had been ordered to rescue the Lost Battalion at any cost, and the cost was huge.

Later, in April 1945, the 442nd was given another daunting task. The German's "Gothic Line" in Italy consisted of fortified mountains that were thought to be impenetrable. The Gothic Line had held even after five months of aerial bombardment and artillery barrages by the Allies. A breakthrough was needed, and the 442nd was assigned the task. The solution was to initiate a surprise attack by scaling a nearly vertical mountainside during the night. Climbing for hours in the dark, they finally reached the top. Then, in only thirty-four minutes, they overran two key enemy outposts on the mountaintop and forced the enemy into retreat. This made it possible for Allied units to advance and opened northern Italy.

One of the most poignant moments may have been the participation of some 442nd soldiers in the liberation of one of the concentration camps at Dachau. As Japanese American soldiers liberated Jews in concentration camps in Germany, their own family members were still being held in detention camps by their own government at home.

The 442nd served in seven major campaigns in Europe and became the most decorated unit for its size and length of service in the history of the United States military. Among other decorations, the 442nd received a Congressional Medal of Honor;

8 Presidential Distinguished Unit Citations; 9,468 Purple Hearts; 18,143 individual decorations; 21 Medals of Honor; and 52 Distinguished Service Crosses. The army chief of staff, General George C. Marshall, said that the men of the 442nd were superb. "They showed rare courage and tremendous fighting spirit . . . everybody wanted them."

When they returned to the United States in July 1946, a reception was held for them in Washington, D.C. President Truman pinned the Presidential Unit Citation on their colors and said: "You fought not only the enemy, but you fought prejudice—and you have won."

Members of the 442nd returned to Hawai'i, and many entered politics and played key roles in establishing equal opportunity for all the people of Hawai'i. Nearly sixty years later, veterans of the 442nd are still active, respected leaders in the community. It has been my privilege to know and work with many of them.

When I think about the tenth Paradoxical Commandment, I remember the courage of my wife, Elizabeth, during the adoption of our children in Romania—especially our youngest child, Angela.

My wife and I flew to Romania in February 1991 to adopt a baby girl. The first Gulf War had just started, and our Pan Am flight had to set down in Zagreb, Yugoslavia, at a time when the country was falling apart. Fortunately, we arrived safely, and with the help of a Romanian doctor who worked with the adoption agency, we found Spencer and Angela. We knew immediately that they were supposed to be our children.

Angela was in a hospital in Bucharest. Her birth family had been too poor to feed her during her first four months, and when she became sick, they abandoned her at the hospital. When we first saw her, she was six months old, only ten or eleven pounds, fighting the last stages of whooping cough, and so congested throughout her head and chest that she had difficulty breathing. Pus was oozing from both her ears. She was bound up in a mummy bag, so she couldn't move her legs. She was given little to eat, so she was underweight. The hospital didn't change her diapers very often, so she had bleeding open sores on her back side.

She didn't move when Elizabeth first held her in her arms. She just looked up with her big eyes, and clasped her hands together as if in prayer. She was stubbornly clinging to life.

I flew home to file the paperwork to adopt two children instead of one. Elizabeth stayed in Bucharest to fight the bureaucratic battle. There was a lot of paperwork, and there were jurisdictional issues between government agencies. Setbacks occurred almost daily. This went on for two months.

Elizabeth knew that Angela was getting no stimulation. The babies in the hospital were not held or taken out of their cribs for exercise. They were not given toys or objects to play with. Even the walls of the hospital were bare, so there was nothing for the children to look at. The babies were just wrapped up and left in their cribs. Every few hours, the nurses would enter the wards and rush around with heavy Fanta bottles with rice gruel, sticking the bottles into the babies' mouths and then rushing back to the lobby to smoke and play cards.

Elizabeth began walking several miles to the hospital every day to see Angela. It was winter, below freezing, and snow and ice covered the streets and sidewalks. But day after day, Elizabeth went to the hospital. She held Angela, and talked to her, and sang to her, and took her over to the window to see the tree outside. Angela began to respond. Her eyes began to scan the tree, and her face changed when Elizabeth spoke to her.

Angela's progress was exciting. Then came despair. Here is what Elizabeth wrote in her journal:

Today I feel sick to my stomach. I went to the hospital to see Angela. When I arrived, they wouldn't let me in. Angela wasn't in her room, where I had visited her so many times before. The dark-haired doctor who speaks a little English said, "Angela is very, very ill. This is serious, very dangerous."

"Where is she?" I asked.

"She is in intensive care. Very serious, very dangerous. You cannot see her. Nobody can see her."

The nurses had told me earlier that Angela was going to die. It was clear that they weren't going to do anything to stop her from dying. "She's going to die before you can adopt her," they had said. "Pick another baby."

All of that was coming back to me now. I asked the dark-haired doctor, "Is she going to die?"

"Talk to Dr. Chikovitch," she said. "Please come back tomorrow."

I was really discouraged. There were no chairs, so I sat on the lobby floor and cried. Then I got up and walked all the way back to the apartment, an hour and a half in the snow and cold. While I walked, I talked to Angela out loud. "Hang in there, Angela. We're going to take you home, so be strong. You'll do fine once we get home, just hang on." I kept repeating those words out loud, all the way back to my apartment.

Later, we learned that the Romanian Commission on Adoptions had given Angela's name to another couple who arrived in Romania long after we did. That couple had apparently made substantial gifts to the commission and the hospital director. The director couldn't make a deal with the other couple if they saw

Elizabeth holding Angela every day, so Angela was put in intensive care to stop Elizabeth from seeing her.

Elizabeth had given her best, and had been kicked in the teeth. But she wasn't about to give up. She pressed on to get the adoption documents, knowing that each day counted. She obtained the court decree of adoption and then went to the hospital to take legal custody of Angela.

When she arrived with the documentation, the hospital director stalled, reluctant to give up Angela. Apparently, she was still trying to work a deal with the other couple. But Elizabeth made it clear that she wasn't leaving without Angela. She stood her ground. The hospital director finally conceded, and Elizabeth walked through the hospital gates with Angela in her arms.

Back in the apartment, Elizabeth made sure that Angela got proper nutrition, an antibiotic provided by our doctor in the United States, and lots of love. Angela improved dramatically in only a few days. The sores healed, the pus disappeared, and Angela's new life began.

Joe Rice, who we encountered earlier, learned early in life that sometimes, just taking a stand can be meaningful, even if you don't win.

At seventeen, and with puberty against me, I was a tall, skinny, scared-of-my-shadow kind of kid. Timid smiles, quiet personality, and a "stay out of it" attitude usually got me through the daily high school events without much notice, until Willy Carter challenged me to my first and only high school fight.

Although he was only a freshman, Willy Carter wrestled in the unlimited weight classification, reserved for those of mammoth size and proportion. He exuded an exaggerated aura of confidence, both physically and emotionally. Willy harassed, but was never harassed. He got away with this behavior on a routine basis. No one wanted to stand up to him and suffer the consequences.

Jenny Bradley was, in my mind, "my girl." It didn't matter that she rarely spoke to me, seldom cast those deep brown eyes upon my freckled face, and never gave me more than a fleeting smile. However, we did sit together on the school bus once, and she lived right across the street.

When I saw Jenny that morning, Willy had her cornered by the lockers and was loudly and descriptively commenting on her well-endowed body and all its lovely contours. Something in me sparked. As I rushed toward them, out came the words "Leave her alone and I mean it!" "Make me, make me, make me!" Willy taunted again and again in a squeaky teasing voice. As his large head and scrunched face moved side to side in mockery, his double chins wobbled this way and that. I should have laughed out loud at the sight just to break the tension, but something in me stood strong and serious.

Caught up in the moment, with a crowd gathering from both ends of the school hallway, Jenny backed out from between us. I asked him again to leave her alone. Suddenly, without warning, Willy rushed me and pinned my almost 146 pounds to the locker. Backing away, he launched a roundhouse swing that connected with the locker and not me. I slipped to the floor, unhurt, as the crowd began to chant "Fight, fight, fight" and "get him, get him, get him." The history teacher, Mr. James, broke things up and gave me the "You know better than to be fighting in the hallway!" warning speech before he left. As we passed in opposite directions down the hallway, Willy mumbled, "After school behind the gym."

Word spread faster than a summer wildfire about the big fight, after school, behind the gym. Knowing of the impending battle, I thought Jenny would bestow encouragement and understanding upon me, her white knight. Instead, silence. After school, in spite of mixed feelings and a nauseous stomach, I found my feet making their way down the polished wooden floor of the hallway, past the gray metal lockers numbered 120, 119, 118, and through double doors.

Outside, I saw the eyes follow me as I made my way around back. I heard the whispers. "Is he going to meet Willy?" "Oh my God, he's going!" "Let's go watch."

I turned the corner to the gym with the speed of an ancient turtle, head down, and ready to retract. Willy and his entourage were waiting. He and his friends were laughing and shooting dice against the gym wall. I don't believe he thought I had the guts, the audacity, to fight him. He calmly picked up his die and coins, returned them to his pocket, and came to meet me.

There was no usual standoff, no facing each other with looks of intimidation. He just walked right up to me and hit me in the head. Down I went. I got up and returned one. I went down again and again after each of his solid hits, finding the strength to get up each time. My arms swung around wildly, large looping swings that began behind my back and rose over my shoulder as they raced toward his face. My fingernails, not my fist, raked across him. For a split second, I thought I had gotten him good, that I had the edge, when one adrenaline-packed punch landed me solidly on the hot black asphalt. He then began kicking, angling so that his kicks would find their way between my legs.

I could hear the kids yelling and screaming as I unconsciously pulled myself back into a standing position. I tried to focus, but my eyes filled with tears and began to close over. I couldn't see too much. I had red stuff on my hands and clothes. I could hear him cursing at me, but I just kept swinging, sometimes connecting, mostly not.

Suddenly, I felt a pair of bulky arms close in as the custodian pulled me back from the fight. Wildly, but with perfect timing, Willy's last kick connected with my groin. I fell to the ground, curled with my own hands between my legs. It hurt!

As we were hauled to the principal's office I had plenty of time to think the worst. I was sitting in the principal's office and Willy was sent to the nurse. He was bleeding all over, his shirt and clothes torn. I could see his white rolls of fat glistening with beads of blood and sweat. I hurt, too, but no one thought I needed to see the nurse, so I just sat there and tried not to cry. I hurt in every conceivable spot.

Although battered, I was optimistic about the possibility that Willy would be kicked out of school, Jenny would appreciate what I had done, and the other kids would be free of Willy. When the principal called me into his office he stared at me for a long time before speaking. This deliberate silence was for my benefit—enough time to realize that everything might not end up so rosy.

"You are a senior! You picked on a freshman," he started.

"At your age there is no excuse for what you've done, simply no excuse at all. You are suspended for a week and I want to see your parents."

I never got a say in my defense. My parents never showed up to talk to the principal and nobody called them, and nobody called me—Jenny, for example.

When I returned to school, my head and chest still hurt and I realized I had clearly lost the fight. But things at school had changed. I had gained instant popularity! In the eyes of the students, I was a winner because nobody expected I would show up, let alone fight. Everyone wanted my take on the fight. Everyone wanted my attention—well, except for Jenny. She was livid the day she met me in the center of the hallway. I had embarrassed her; my interference in her life had been unneeded, unwanted, and stupid.

Willy was also a different person. Aside from the obvious patchwork of fine crisscrossed lines and scabs on his face, he went through campus as unnoticed as someone "unlimited" can after that. Willy never regained his command over those he deemed the weakest or most insignificant. Gone were his days of unchallenged harassing. Although he was victorious in the physical battle, I suspect he lost a lot more on other levels. Lives were definitely changed that day.

I came to understand in the weeks and months to follow that some things are worth caring about and worth a "beating" if that's what it takes. I understood, deep inside, that on that day I had made a decision to take control of my life and do something. I had known that Willy would hurt me, that the principal would punish me, that Jenny was not interested in me, and that my parents wouldn't care enough to pick me up from the principal's office. In the scope of events in the world this was a small thing. In my life it was monumental. I had done the right thing. I had stood up to a bully. That planted a seed that would soon grow and alter how I dealt with more serious issues throughout my life.

The men of the 442nd held back nothing. Their motto, "Go for Broke," symbolized that total commitment. The world treated them and their families badly, but they gave the world their best, anyway. Elizabeth gave her best while trying to help Angela. When she got kicked in the teeth, she gave even more. Joe Rice gave his best by standing up to a campus bully. He got beaten and punished, but it was the beginning of his lifelong habit of giving his best, anyway.

When you give your best, you are saying something about who you are: You are the kind of person who draws upon *all* your energy and talent and intelligence to do what needs to be done. You are the kind of person who doesn't hold back. You do your best, regardless of whether you will be appreciated, or rewarded, or attacked, or ignored. Doing your best is part of your character.

You can't control what everybody else does, but you can control your own behavior. Doing your best defines you. If you aren't doing your best, you aren't who you are supposed to be. You aren't all that you *can* be. Remember that you are unique. You have something special to contribute. Why would you want to hold back?

One of my favorite questions is this: *If you aren't giving the world your best, what world are you saving it for?* Every day, each of us can give our very best, and enjoy the personal meaning that comes to us when we do so.

Am I living the tenth Paradoxical Commandment?

1. How do I feel when I give the world my best?
2. How do I feel when I don't give the world my best?
3. Have I ever given the world the best I have and gotten kicked in the teeth? How did that make me feel?

4. What are the reasons I wouldn't do it again?
5. What are the reasons I *would* do it again?

6. The biggest men and women
with the biggest ideas can be shot down
by the smallest men and women
with the smallest minds.
Think big anyway.

Part Three:

❧

Making a Difference

7. People favor underdogs but follow only top dogs.
Fight for a few underdogs anyway.

8. What you spend years
building may be destroyed overnight.
Build anyway.

Changing the World

If you live the Paradoxical Commandments, you will change the world. You will love people, and do good, and succeed, and be honest and frank, and think big, and fight for underdogs, and build, and help people, and give the world your best. When you do those things, you will have a positive impact on the people, organizations, and communities around you. They will change, you will change, and the world will change—for the better.

I wrote the Paradoxical Commandments to encourage people to make the world a better place. I wanted to help people get past their excuses, their difficult past, their difficult present, so they could find personal meaning and *make a difference anyway*.

There are so many things that need doing—so many problems to solve, so many opportunities to seize. Some of the problems and opportunities seem so big that it may be hard to believe that one person can make a difference. The world is just too crazy! And yet, nothing will get better unless each of us decides to make a difference *anyway*.

Spiritually Liberated, Personally Committed

The people who are most likely to change the world are people who are both spiritually liberated and personally committed to making life better for others. This is the practical importance of living the Paradoxical Commandments. When you live the Paradoxical Commandments, you will be liberated from all the forces and events that you can't control. You will be liberated from your excuses, your difficult past, or your difficult present. You will not be locked in to "getting ahead," and will be ready to "get meaning" instead.

The meaning in your life will come from being personally committed to loving and helping people, and doing what is right and good and true. It will come from being fully engaged in the world, becoming part of something larger than yourself and focusing on others. The personal meaning and deep happiness will not come from withdrawing into a safe garden and ignoring the needs of those around you. It will come from living a fully committed life.

When you become spiritually liberated and personally committed, what do you do?

Fortunately, what needs to be done in the world is clear. Most people agree on what they want out of life. They want the basics—food, clothing, shelter, good health. They want a beautiful and healthy natural environment. They want opportunities— education, jobs, and personal growth. They want human dignity and a spiritual life. They want love. They want peace.

What is so crazy is that most of these needs *can* be met, but we are not meeting them. We live in a world in which hundreds of millions live without adequate food, clothing, or shelter. Hundreds of millions are sick and live in poor environments, without the opportunity for a good education, jobs, or personal growth. Hundreds of millions struggle for human dignity and spiritual growth. There is not enough love, not enough peace.

It doesn't have to be this way. *There are no laws of science or human nature that are preventing us from dramatically improving the world for all of us.* There is no shortage of intelligence or resources.

The roadblocks are in our heads and hearts. There are historical animosities, as well as political and cultural differences, that run deep and are difficult to overcome. Attitudes are hard to change. But they *can* change. It takes time and effort. It takes education, negotiation, and the building of mutual understanding. But it can be done. And it is worth doing.

How can I get started?

1. What problems or issues trouble me or excite me the most?
2. Have I studied the problems or issues? How can I learn more?
3. Who is already working on these problems? What can I do?
4. Who can I invite to join me?
5. Can we start in our own neighborhood, or city, or state?
6. When are we going to get started?

Don't Worry about How Big a Difference

When you see a way to make a difference by loving people, or doing good, or succeeding, or being honest and frank, or thinking big, or fighting for the underdog, or building, or helping people, or giving your best—do it. Do it because it gives you meaning and happiness. Don't worry about *how big* a difference it will make. The impact of your actions may be hard to judge in advance. In fact, you may never know all the impacts. You don't need to. All you need to know is that you are living the paradoxical life, and you have done something meaningful.

Paul Katz tells the story of something he did that was simple for him but had a big impact on the life of a young man.

He must have been twelve years old that first summer, about twenty-five years ago. I was fresh out of college, working as the director of a YMCA summer wilderness camp program for preadolescents. Gavin was an active, skinny kid with a mischievous quick wit and the propensity to be in the wrong place at the wrong time.

Our camp repeated a three-week program a few times

during the course of the summer. Gavin was there all day, every day, all summer long. Over the course of those long summer days, it seemed that he learned every handhold and foothold of the rock faces we climbed, every rapid of the rivers we canoed, and every inch of the Appalachian Trail in Connecticut we hiked. He knew all the rules and, in the spirit of fun and mischief, knew how to break them without causing concern for safety. I remember him as one of those kids that I grew to enjoy, but always, *always* kept a close eye on. I knew he would push the limit and test my authority, but I gave him freedom and room to explore anyway.

Coming into camp on the last night of our third and final weeklong backpack trip together, I noticed a hawk feather off to the side of the trail. The symbol of strength, grace, and natural beauty struck me at the time as the perfect way to acknowledge Gavin's participation in the program. The next morning, in a simple but serious ceremony, my co-leader and I presented him with the feather. We hiked out that day, and I'm not sure I thought about the feather again.

Twenty years later, I was working at a YMCA in western Massachusetts. In my leadership role, I was never surprised to be called to the member service desk to meet a prospective member. I was surprised, however, when the person across the desk from me looked at me and my name tag and said, "You are Paul Katz. Did you used to work in Westport, Connecticut? I'm Gavin."

I was astounded. His face was unmistakable, but he was more than six feet tall! In my mind's eye, of course, he was still the skinny little kid I remembered.

Gavin told me that that summer in the wilderness camp had been a turning point in his life. He had just finished his graduate degree in social work, and attributed his career choice to the lessons he learned with me on the trail.

"Do you remember the hawk feather you gave me at the end of camp?" he asked. I did recall the simple ceremony all those years ago. "I still have it," he said, explaining that it has traveled with him and always has a special spot in his bedroom. He asked if he could bring his new wife to the Y to meet me. She knew all about the hawk feather. She had heard about his time in the wilderness and had heard stories about me. I was honored in an indescribable way as I told Gavin I looked forward to meeting his wife.

Paul learned a valuable lesson: an action that seems small to us can have a big impact on somebody else. "The gift I received from Gavin that day taught me that we must support, challenge, and guide the lives of young people," Paul says. "They may not show their appreciation, or even acknowledge our efforts. In fact, we may never know if we've made an impact. But we should support, challenge, and guide them, anyway."

Do I know how big a difference I can make?

1. Can I recall a small act of kindness or recognition that made a big impact on me?
2. Can I recall a small act of my own that made a big impact on somebody else?
3. What small act of kindness or recognition can I carry out today? Tomorrow?

Don't Think You Have Too Little to Offer

Making a difference is something that each of us can do, no matter what our ability or condition. Stu Gothold learned this at a school that he visited once.

During the time I was Los Angeles County Superintendent of Schools, one of the responsibilities of our office was
to supervise one of the largest special education regional
programs in the country. We had about twelve thousand very
severely handicapped children in a variety of school programs throughout Los Angeles County.

It was my practice to visit schools on a pretty regular
basis. I remember a visit I made one day to Lincoln School
in San Gabriel Valley, which was a school dedicated totally
to the most severely handicapped and fragile children. These
children were so fragile medically and physically that over
the course of a year usually three or four of them would
pass away. So we had a constant concern about the mental
health of our staff and faculty as well as the well-being of
the children themselves. I would spend time there supporting the staff and telling them how much we appreciated the
work they were doing.

I was touring the school with the assistant principal, and
we went into a classroom. Classrooms in the school usually
had only three or four children because they required such
constant attention. In this classroom there was a youngster
who was strapped to a gurney board that was upright and
padded in the shape of the youngster's body. He was held
to the gurney board with straps that covered most of his

torso and limbs. He was so fragile and his bones were so weak that he didn't have any control over his skeleton and muscular functions.

While we were in the classroom, there were two adults working with the youngster. One adult was literally teaching the youngster how to eat. The youngster was probably between seven and nine years old, but he needed to be retaught basic life functions on a daily basis. I was fascinated by watching this adult work with the youngster, and take him through the steps of the act of eating. She was using a sugar cube on a spoon, working with the muscles of his face and mouth and throat, and teaching him how to swallow the cube of sugar.

I turned to the assistant principal and I said, "You know, I've seen a lot of good teaching in my day, but this may be one of the finest examples of teaching that I have seen in a long time. My compliments to the teacher."

The assistant principal turned to me and said, "That's not the teacher."

And I said, "Really? That's hard to believe. It's such an exquisite act of teaching."

And she said, "No, and it's not the teacher aid, either."

"You're kidding. Well, who is it?" I asked.

"Well, it's a former student of the program," she said.

"We have a feeling here that if we can get the students in this program to move to the limits of their potential, then they can be productive citizens. One of the ways we try to do that is to have them come back and help us in the program. This is one of the people we call a 'Special Aide.' We have a special set of requirements so that we can go outside the usual hiring practices and have people like this work with us in the program."

Whatever our condition, whatever our talent or ability, each of us can make a difference.

I remember a situation in which I knew so little that it opened up an opportunity for me to help others. I was a law clerk during the summer of 1975 at the Tokyo office of an international law firm. The lawyers there were mostly Americans serving as advisors on U.S. law.

I was one of five law clerks, and the other four were far ahead of me in their Japanese language ability. I was assigned to translate Japanese legal documents, which included a lot of specialized and archaic legal terms. I sat there, day after day, surrounded by dictionaries, looking up words. It was tedious, painstaking work.

Because I knew that I was likely to come across the same terms again and again in other documents, I decided to write down the definition of each new term as I went along. By the end of the summer, I had created a small dictionary of Japanese legal terms and their English translations. I gave it to the senior partner, suggesting that it might be helpful to law clerks in the future. He was delighted. He thumbed through the pages and then turned to me and smiled. "You turned a shortcoming into a contribution," he said simply.

In small ways or big, each of us can find a way to make a difference. Sometimes, in discovering how to make the best of a bad situation, we discover how to make things better for others, and derive personal meaning in the process.

Do I know what I have to offer?

1. Do I have a unique skill or hobby? Can I use it to make a difference?
2. Do I have the patience to do things that others won't do? Can I use that personal quality to make a difference?
3. Do I have a shortcoming or limitation that I can turn into a contribution?

What We Need Is Each Other

The power to bring about change is in our hands. That's because the most important thing that each of us needs is *each other*. Many of our social problems stem from our lack of attention to each other—in early childhood, to stimulate growth; in our schools, to draw out the unique potential of each individual; in our communities, to help our friends and neighbors. Many of our problems have grown out of our alienation—our inattention to each other as individuals. And that is something we have the power to change. One by one, person by person, we can make a difference.

Taking care of people is not just the government's job. It's everybody's job. And it's not just about money—it's about giving our time and talent freely to enjoy the uniqueness of others and attend to their needs. When we begin to give this individual attention, one by one, as a gift to each other, our society will begin to right itself.

It will be like the miracle of the loaves and the fishes. Just when we think that we have very little, we will discover that we have a nearly infinite supply of what each of us needs the most—

love, acceptance, family, community. We will discover that our baskets are full, and always have been, and always will be, if we only care enough to give what is in them—our time, our talent, our attention, our love.

Challenging the Status Quo

One of the biggest obstacles to positive change is the drive for success. Since success is usually defined in terms of the status quo, the desire for success leads people to conform. There are exceptions, of course, but for most people, succeeding in the world of organizations means playing the game—not rocking the boat but working in established ways to achieve established rewards. Depending on how the system is structured, it may even be advantageous for individuals to exploit problems instead of solving them.

To challenge the whole system is to risk becoming an outcast, isolated and not eligible for the rewards the system distributes. For that reason, people usually stick with the traditional way of doing things, even when the traditional way has become wrong or irrelevant. Following the accepted rules is the way to power, wealth, and fame, even if it's not the way to solve society's problems.

We need champions of fundamental change. We may not find many among those who are enamored with success. We are more likely to find them among those who focus on meaning instead. As Albert Einstein said, "Try not to become a man of success but rather try to become a man of value." People of value, who care about others, are positioned to be champions of positive changes that will benefit the world around them.

Taking a Stand

A lot of problems exist because people are reluctant to stand up and speak out. They are unwilling to challenge traditional rules and assumptions, even though they know the rules don't work and the assumptions are wrong.

Of course, most people don't stand up and speak out because they know or fear that they will get punished. Often, rebels are stripped of their symbols of "success"—their power and position. This is never pleasant, but it's not the end of the world for people who are focused on meaning. In fact, it can be the *beginning* of the world for them—the beginning of something more important than success, the beginning of great personal meaning and deep happiness.

Scott Lewis, a Jesuit priest and professor, decided to take a stand. He shares his transformation after the tragedy of September 11, 2001, and the scandals in the Catholic church:

My personal journey had been blessed with many enriching experiences, one of which was the opportunity to work with Mother Teresa's Sisters for several years. I was always amazed at her determination in the face of insurmountable obstacles and the joyful vision of love for the world's poor that energized her work. Responding to accusations that her work was insignificant and ineffectual in the face of so much suffering and poverty, she always replied that she was called to be faithful, not successful. She was truly a master of the "anyway" principle! I was not surprised when I saw the Paradoxical Commandments hanging on the wall at her children's home.

I learned a lot from Mother Teresa and her Sisters, perhaps more than I was aware of at the time. In the last year and a half I have begun to learn the meaning of the "anyway" principle. For me, it has meant the difference between total despair and a meaningful life.

My life began to change on 9/11. I had spent the whole

day in front of the TV transfixed by the unfolding horror and devastation of the attacks on the World Trade Center and the Pentagon. I was in a state of shock. At four o'clock, I walked into the classroom to give my first lecture of the fall semester at the theological faculty where I am a professor of New Testament. The course was my favorite, the Gospel of John, and I had been teaching it regularly for several years.

But that afternoon, I did not want to be there. The topic seemed so empty and mundane in light of what had happened. It seemed to me that religion itself had contributed to the atmosphere of hatred and intolerance that had just vented its fury on so many innocent victims. I had been shocked and dismayed by the dark side of religion during a two-year assignment in Jerusalem. Now, 9/11 seemed to confirm my disillusionment.

Walking into that classroom was very difficult, but I had to go. I began the class with a prayer, and then shared how I felt. I proposed to make the experience of 9/11 the lens through which we would study and interpret the message of John. Then I began. The semester's journey unveiled depths of the gospel that I didn't know existed. It was one of my most successful semesters, but more importantly, it set me on a new course.

Over the next few months, I struggled with my vocation as a priest and as an academic. Gradually an awareness and conviction began to grow in me that in order for my work to be truly legitimate and meaningful, it had to contribute to a new world and a new religious understanding.

But there was more to come. The sexual abuse scandal in the Roman Catholic church exploded. As revelations and charges continued to mount, I felt my own calling shaken. I was embarrassed to let people know that I was a priest, and I questioned whether I wanted to belong to a disgraced profession. Yes, I know that the scandal did not involve all or even a majority of priests. But a secretive and rigidly hierarchical structure had contributed to the situation.

I wanted to do something for the healing and renewal of the church, but what and how? True healing and renewal means a change in the system. I felt strongly that this change would include a willingness to put into practice openness, equality, accountability, and the sharing of ministries. In order for my preaching and teaching to contribute to this, I would need a change in myself.

I resolved to speak and write the truth, painful though it might be and regardless of who might raise objections, and to avoid echoing the party line. And that is a fearful thing. What will people say? Will I be opposed or condemned?

Run afoul of authority? Lose my job? And what good will it really accomplish? Once again, the only answer that seemed reasonable was "Do it anyway!" I might not ever see the results personally, but that should not be of any concern to me.

Over the past year, I have tried to put this into practice in the classroom and the pulpit. Sometimes fear can be powerful. At times I have beaten a hasty retreat into the security of the acceptable. But more often than not, I have found new strength and purpose and my voice has become bolder. During my homily at the celebration of Holy Thursday last year, I spoke of the church's pain and my hopes and dreams for a transformed and changed church for the future. It was a painful and moving experience, and not one that I would wish to have every day. But I discovered that people are more receptive than I expected. I have received a lot of support. Many had similar thoughts and feelings, and were waiting for someone to voice them. But I'm trying the Mother Teresa approach—striving to be faithful rather than successful. It seems to me that "anyway" is another word for faith.

It can be a struggle to determine what we should do, and how we should do it. But if enough of us decide to make a difference anyway, the context and content of our decisions will change. If many of us raise our voices, there will be a chorus, and it will be heard.

Am I ready and willing to take a stand?

1. Am I satisfied with things as they are? Why? Why not?
2. If not, what can I improve?
3. What do I feel so strongly about that I am willing to take a stand, even if it costs me to do so?
4. Am I ready to take that stand now? Am I willing to speak up? Organize others? Write fliers, pamphlets, and letters to the editor?
5. Am I willing to be known and judged by the stand that I take?

Start at Home and at Work

How do we begin this process of change? We start with ourselves, at home and at work. We start with our daily decisions.

People who are focused on "success" and people who are focused on meaning ask different questions when they make decisions in their daily lives and work. For example, a power-oriented individual may ask: Will this make me look good? Will this enhance my power? Will this give me the visibility I want? Will this be an incredibly effective way to stick it to my chief rival? Will this improve my relationship with my boss? Will this position me better for my next promotion?

A meaning-oriented individual will ask a different set of questions: Whose needs will this meet? Are there greater needs that should be addressed before this one? In meeting this need, who will suffer negative impacts? How can we mitigate those negative impacts? Is this decision consistent with the values and goals of my organization? Is it consistent with my own values and ethics? These questions will lead to better decisions, because they address the needs of others, not the power or visibility of the decision maker.

In addition to better decisions, we can change the way we behave, and how we spend our time. We can become public citizens and volunteers who are actively speaking, writing, organizing, and working to make things better.

It's not easy. We're all busy with work, families, obligations. And we're not sure we can make much of a difference anyway. Life is short. Why complicate it?

That may be what my wife, Elizabeth, was thinking as she sat at her PTA board meeting. The department of education had informed parents that it planned to eliminate the sixth grade at the elementary school our children attended. The students would go to a middle school, instead. Informally, parents were told that there was no use protesting the decision. It was presented as a fait accompli, a done deal. There had been no discussion with parents, no involvement by the school-based management council, no explanation of the decision, and no evidence to support the decision. The department of education was just going to do it.

Elizabeth had been unable to attend the previous PTA board meeting because she was on a business trip. Now, she looked at her fellow board members and asked: Why is the sixth grade going to be eliminated? How will it be better for our children? What do the parents think of this? Isn't the PTA board supposed to represent the parents?

Again, she was told that the decision had been made. It was a done deal. But Elizabeth decided to make a difference *anyway*. She got the board to agree to survey the parents. She prepared the survey form, which went home in the children's backpacks. The results? Nearly every family in the school completed the survey, and 90 percent said they were opposed to the elimination of the sixth grade. Teachers also expressed their concerns about the proposed change.

What to do next? Elizabeth formed an ad hoc committee of parents to study the issue. She included on the committee a number of parents who were teachers or had advanced degrees, so the committee could draw on their expertise in education and research. The committee drafted an issue paper, identifying eight issues that needed to be addressed before a decision should be made on eliminating the sixth grade.

As the committee members did their research, they became more concerned. When the district superintendent came to an afternoon meeting at the school, Elizabeth and other parents shared their concerns. He was unable to explain why the change would be better for the children. He gave the parents a month to present information to him that might change his mind.

That gave the parents little time. They pressed ahead with their meetings and their research and completed their issue paper within a month. Copies were delivered to parents, the district superintendent, and board of education members. It was none too soon. The district superintendent had already moved the issue to a committee of the board of education, not waiting for the information from the parents.

Then came a crucial two weeks. On Monday, the parents testified before the education committee of the board of education; on Tuesday and Wednesday, they testified at hearings at the state legislature on a resolution that addressed the issue; on Thursday, they testified before the full board of education. The following Monday, they met with the lieutenant governor; and on Wednesday, they presented their case at a neighborhood board meeting. The next Monday, they held an open meeting of all the parents at the school, to debate the issues and take a stand. Elizabeth and the committee reported on their findings and activities and received the unanimous support of all 175 parents who attended the meeting.

In the end, the board of education, state legislature, and neighborhood board all agreed with the parents that there was insufficient evidence to support the change. It was agreed that the decision would not be made until the department of education could prove that the change would be good for the children.

In only two months, the parents had organized, conducted research, prepared an issue paper, argued their position at a series of public meetings, and succeeded in reversing a decision that was "a done deal." It was an intense period of telephoning, meeting, testifying, and following up. The parents on the committee had jobs and children who needed their time. But they stayed up late at night to discuss the issues, find relevant studies, prepare the issue paper, deliver copies of the issue paper, and attend meetings. They carved time out of their busy schedules to take a serious look at a decision affecting their children.

It began with one voice: Elizabeth's. It began with one question: Is this best for our children? From there it grew, and more voices and questions were raised.

Elizabeth had no experience as a "community organizer." She had never drafted an issue paper or testified before the legislature. But she had the courage to stand up and speak out about a decision made by "the system," and she attracted others who were willing to do the same. The result was that the "done deal" was undone.

*Am I ready to start working on a problem
or issue that's right in front of me?*

1. Is there a problem or issue that is affecting me or a member of my family right now?

2. Is there a problem or issue that is affecting me or my colleagues at work right now?
3. Can I get involved and do something about it?
4. What do I need to know?
5. Who should I talk to? Whose support do I need?
6. What steps should I take?
7. What is a reasonable timetable?

Becoming Public Citizens and Volunteers

The world will change when more and more people carve out time from their busy schedules to raise questions, challenge assumptions, set high standards, and pitch in to help each other. The meaning that people find in their work and families will be magnified by the meaning they find as community leaders, public citizens, and volunteers.

After a distinguished academic and public policy career, Dr. Stephen S. Weiner retired and became a public citizen. He became a senior advisor for Civic Ventures, a national nonprofit organization whose goal is to increase the civic involvement of older Americans. He cofounded a leadership symposium for campus chief executive officers. And he began to speak out about the looming crisis in higher education in California. "A surge in the number of high school graduates in California has begun to outstrip the capacity of California colleges and universities, both public and private, to educate them," says Steve. "It is projected that in the year 2011 alone, six hundred thousand students will not find a place available to them in higher education. Two-thirds of them will not be able to enroll in the classes they need at community colleges, which are suffering severe budget cuts. Most of these students will come from low-income families and a very strong majority will be students of color, especially Latinos. Many of them would be the first in their families to attend college."

The state of California has no plan to educate these students, so Steve and his colleagues launched the Campaign for College Opportunity to generate the political will to get the job done. Their first priority is a statewide drive to inform the public of the problem and its importance. Steve is drawing upon a lifetime of experience in public policy and higher education to open up opportunities for the next generation.

Millions of Americans find meaning by participating in the daily work of nonprofit organizations. Immense good is being done by tens of thousands of organizations such as the YMCA, Salvation Army, and Catholic Charities, as well as service clubs like Rotary, Lions, Kiwanis, and Exchange. Nonprofit organizations have a public purpose and private flexibility. They are about people pitching in to make things better in our communities. Some have an international impact.

A good example is the polio eradication program launched by Rotary International in 1985. At the time the program started, polio was common throughout the world. Rotary decided to save the world's children from this disease and eradicate polio. Since then, Rotarians and their partner agencies have immunized more than two billion children and reduced polio from 350,000 cases in 1988 to fewer than 1,900 in 2002. It is estimated that more than four million children who might have contracted polio have been saved from the disease. Rotarians have raised more than $500 million, and many have traveled to other countries to assist directly in distributing the polio vaccine. As a politically neutral nonprofit organization, Rotary International was the perfect vehicle to work on a humanitarian project that crossed national borders. This volunteer effort has had a huge, tangible impact. When they started, Rotarians must have seen the eradication of polio as an overwhelming task. But they decided to make a difference *anyway*. They are only a few years away from complete victory.

Greg Kemp is a successful real estate developer who volunteers his time to build homes for families in other countries. He says:

It all started when my wife, Annie, and I were traveling by train in mainland China. People along the railroad tracks were huddled late at night around an open fire pit. Their homes were in a garbage dump, built from scrap materials. Seeing them had a big impact on me. What hope do they have? What will happen to their children?

The sight continued to haunt me. A few months later, we were driving near Coeur d'Alene, Idaho, and saw a billboard for Habitat for Humanity. I was curious, so the next day I visited its website. I liked what I saw and immediately signed us up for a Habitat Global Village team that was going to Manukau, New Zealand, an area populated mostly by Maori. We went there and built a home in three weeks. There were eighteen of us, including a judge from New York, a nurse from Alaska, a flight attendant from Florida, a school teacher from Chicago, a retired Episcopalian priest from New Mexico, and an insurance administrator from New Hampshire. The youngest was thirteen, and the oldest was eighty-two.

Next, we signed up for a Habitat Global Village team in the Monteverde cloud forest in Costa Rica. We built two homes in three weeks. We took two teens from the United States and Canada to that project. The teens were in need of a life-changing experience, and they got it.

We travel to areas of the world with disease and strange-looking bugs. We might get a clean change of clothes once a week. We get blisters on our hands, and many sore body parts. But there are all those hugs from the local families for whom we are building new homes. We know we have made the world a better place for them to live. We know we have shown people all over the world that we are willing not only to write a check, but to pick up a hammer. I hope that some day, Habitat will be able to build homes for the families along that railroad line in China.

Judy Asman wanted to be a medical missionary ever since she was ten years old and read an article in *Reader's Digest* about medical missionaries in Ecuador. After a career as a nurse and a hospital administrator, she made her dream come true in 1999, when she joined the Aloha Medical Mission to Laos. She remembers it vividly:

> The mission lasted two weeks, including travel, set up, and five days of surgery. There were thirty-two doctors, nurses, and staff, and each of us donated our time and travel expenses to get there. We went to a small, dirt-road town in northern Laos, to a village with a small, one-story hospital. We brought in some of our own equipment and medicine.

Hundreds of people came out of the mountains, lined up, and camped out near the hospital while we were there. They were from tribal clans. We took stuffed animals and toys for the kids to play with while they were waiting. We also took used clothing and bags of school supplies to give away.

We did two days' triage. We tried to find people who needed surgeries that we could perform that would heal while we were there, so they wouldn't need follow-up care after we were gone. We did surgeries on cleft lips, burns, and goiters. The surgeons operated from 7:00 A.M. to 11:00 P.M., because there were so many people who needed help. I did incisions, drainage of abscesses, antibiotics, sutures, postoperative care. In just five days we provided medical and surgical care for over five hundred people. It was totally exhausting and deeply satisfying.

Why did I go? I went to be a caring presence. I wanted the Laotians to know that there are kind and gentle people in the world who care about them, and will come to help them without expecting anything in return. They were such lovely people! They were so gracious, so grateful and giving, even though they were very poor and malnourished. I learned from them. They opened up my eyes to another world.

The Paradoxical Commandments
Action Checklist

1. *People are illogical, unreasonable, and self-centered. Love them anyway.*

   Which illogical, unreasonable, or self-centered people am I going to love anyway?

2. *If you do good, people will accuse you of selfish ulterior motives. Do good anyway.*

   What good things am I going to do, even though people will accuse me of selfish ulterior motives?

3. *If you are successful, you will win false friends and true enemies. Succeed anyway.*

   In what ways am I going to be successful, even though I know I will win false friends and true enemies?

4. *The good you do today will be forgotten tomorrow. Do good anyway.*

   What good things am I committed to doing, even though they will be forgotten tomorrow?

5. *Honesty and frankness make you vulnerable. Be honest and frank anyway.*

With whom, and about what, am I going to be honest, even though it will make me vulnerable?

6. *The biggest men and women with the biggest ideas can be shot down by the smallest men and women with the smallest minds. Think big anyway.*

   What big idea am I going to pursue, even though it will be shot down by small men and women?

7. *People favor underdogs but follow only top dogs. Fight for a few underdogs anyway.*

   Which underdogs am I going to fight for?

8. *What you spend years building may be destroyed overnight. Build anyway.*

   What am I going to build, even though it may be destroyed overnight?

9. *People really need help but may attack you if you do help them. Help people anyway.*

   Who am I going to help, even though they may attack me?

10. *Give the world the best you have and you'll get kicked in the teeth. Give the world the best you have anyway.*

    Am I committed to always giving the world my best, even if I get kicked in the teeth?

Working for change may or may not be the road to "success." But it is a road filled with meaning and deep happiness. People who understand that fact will lead the way. They will not be worried about personal success; they will be worried about saving millions of lives and eventually the life of the planet itself.

Raising the Next Generation

In the *Earthsea* series, Ursula LeGuin chronicles the tale of Ged, the boy who became a wizard and traveled throughout the land, fighting evil. After many adventures, he fought a final battle against a powerful evil. He won, but the battle left him exhausted. He had used up all his magical powers in the cause of good and had become a mere mortal. He started a new life as a goatherd on a hillside in his homeland, living with the woman he loved, raising the child who would become the new wizard. He discovered meaning and satisfaction that he had never known during his years as a "dragon lord" and "archmage."

If we, too, exhaust ourselves in the fight for what is right and good and true, there will be new meaning and satisfaction for us as well. And we can raise the new wizards who will fight the good fight after we are gone.

Gandhi said that "satisfaction lies in the effort, not in the attainment. Full effort is full victory." The paradoxical life is a life of full effort. You can change the world by loving people, doing good, succeeding, being honest and frank, thinking big, fighting for underdogs, building, helping people, and giving the world your best. You can change the world and find personal meaning and deep happiness at the same time. You can make a difference by just deciding to *do it anyway*.

Don't wait to make a difference. Do it now.

The world may be crazy, but it doesn't *have* to be!

9. People really need help but may
attack you if you do help them.
Help people anyway.

Part Four:

An Interview with
Kent Keith

10. Give the world the best you have and you'll
get kicked in the teeth.
Give the world the best you have anyway.

As I have traveled across the country, I have enjoyed meeting thousands of people from all walks of life. During our interactions, they have asked me lots of questions about the Paradoxical Commandments. Here are my answers to the questions I have been asked most frequently.

What is a paradox?

A paradox is something that seems contradictory or against common sense, but turns out to be true.

What is paradoxical about the Paradoxical Commandments?

The paradox is that even when the world around you is not going well, you can still find personal meaning and deep happiness. You can find them by facing the worst in the world with the best in yourself. That seems contradictory, but it is true.

Why is it true?

It is true because personal meaning and deep happiness don't depend on the external factors that you can't control. They depend on your inner life, the part of your life that you *can* control.

The Paradoxical Commandments are about loving people, helping people, and doing what is right and good and true. That's where you can find personal meaning and deep happiness, even when the world around you is difficult.

Why did you write the original ten Paradoxical Commandments in 1968?

I wanted to send a message to student leaders.

I was involved in student government in high school, and when I went to college, I carried that interest with me. During my college years, I was a part-time national consultant for high school student councils. I wrote three booklets and gave more than one hundred speeches in eight different states at high schools, state student council conventions, and student leadership workshops.

The Paradoxical Commandments were part of the first booklet I wrote for student leaders, entitled *The Silent Revolution: Dynamic Leadership in the Student Council.* The booklet was published by Harvard Student Agencies and later by the National Association of Secondary School Principals. About twenty-five to thirty thousand copies were sold or distributed between 1968 and 1972.

During the late sixties, when I was in college, there was a lot of turmoil on college and high school campuses. It was a time of passion and idealism, but also confrontation and conflict.

I saw a lot of idealistic young people go out into the world to do what they thought was right and good and true, only to come back a short time later discouraged or even embittered. They were ready to give up because change was very slow and they didn't get the results they hoped for, and also because nobody seemed to appreciate them.

I wanted change, too, but in my writing and speaking during the sixties, I encouraged students to work with each other, and work through the system, to achieve change. I didn't say it would be easy. I told them it took sustained effort, and the sustained effort needed to be motivated by a genuine concern for others. I told them that if they were going to change the world, they had to really love people, because change took time and love was the only motivation strong enough to keep them going.

I also said that if they did what was right and good and true, they would find meaning and satisfaction, and that meaning and satisfaction would be enough. Recognition and appreciation were nice, but not necessary. If they had the meaning, they didn't need the glory.

I laid down the Paradoxical Commandments as a challenge. The challenge is to always do what is right and good and true, even if others don't appreciate it. You have to keep striving, no matter what, because if you don't, many of the things that need to be done in our world will never get done.

Where were you when you wrote the Paradoxical Commandments?

I was a sophomore at Harvard University in Cambridge, Massachusetts. I lived on the fifth floor of the "I" staircase at Eliot House, a large student residence hall. Several of us lived in the suite. We shared a living room and had our own bedrooms. My bedroom was a gable, like an attic room, and I loved it. It was just big enough for a bed, a dresser, and a desk. I had a portable red Royal Safari manual typewriter, and I used it to write my term papers, my letters, and my first booklet for student leaders, which included the Paradoxical Commandments. I typed the Paradoxical Commandments there at my desk in my attic room at Eliot House.

Did the Paradoxical Commandments come to you all at once, or did you write them over time?

I wrote them during several sittings over a period of time, possibly as long as two months. I usually write by aggregation, gradually building and revising as I go along. In the case of the

Paradoxical Commandments, I sat down and tried to think of the things that can be difficult in life. Those things became the statements of adversity that begin each commandment. Then I thought of the positive commandments to attach to each of these difficult situations. I wanted to create a "jolt" in the reader by placing a positive commandment right after each statement of adversity. I also wanted to make it clear that the positive commandments override the adversity. I did that by ending each commandment with the word "anyway."

Why are there ten Paradoxical Commandments?

I grew up in a Christian environment, so I thought that if I was going to have commandments, there should be ten of them. After all, there was a precedent for ten. When I got to ten, I stopped writing.

Have you ever thought of adding any new commandments?

No. I think that the original ten cover a broad range of situations. I have never felt the need to add any new ones.

You were only nineteen when you wrote the Paradoxical Commandments. How did you have that much wisdom at such a young age?

At the time I wrote the Paradoxical Commandments, I didn't think I was writing wisdom. I was just describing the fundamental values that I had learned from my parents and my church, and the meaning that I had already experienced from living those values. I was issuing a challenge to live the way I thought most of us know that we should live. You could say that I wasn't inventing—I was reporting. I was reporting what I had already learned to be true.

When I was growing up, the concepts of honor and duty and loyalty and love and truth were not heroic concepts to me—they were everyday stuff. They were the values my parents lived, and the values I was expected to live by, too. That is why it was a special pleasure to include the story about my father in *Anyway: The Paradoxical Commandments*. The story of his defense of the sergeant who was wrongfully accused of stealing is only one example of the way my parents have lived their values. They don't think of themselves as heroes, just as people trying to live and love and do what's right. They know that doing what is right means taking risks, and there might be a price to pay. So be it. I have always been proud of my parents, and I think that is one of their most important gifts to me—being the kind of people I have always been proud of.

When I was growing up, I not only learned values, I learned that the most fundamental values are universal. I learned it from being raised in California, Virginia, Rhode Island, and Hawai'i. I learned it by going to nine schools in twelve years. I also learned it from books. Again, my parents promoted this kind of learning. I remember one summer when I was in elementary school, we traveled across the country, moving from one Marine Corps assignment to the next. When Sunday came, my parents pulled out a book on the world's major religions. So there I was, learning about Judaism, Hinduism, Buddhism, and Islam, as well as Christianity, and I began to notice some common themes. The differences between religions are important, but so are the similarities.

There are several specific events that I describe in my first book that I think help to explain how I could have written the Paradoxical Commandments when I was only nineteen. When I was fifteen, I spoke up on a student council issue and was attacked and even picketed. And then when I was eighteen, I was literally run out of town in the Midwest for speaking honestly and frankly to a group of student leaders at a workshop. Those were situations that caused me to think about what I stood for, and what was worth doing, and how I could find meaning, even if the results weren't what I had hoped for.

I also learned from an old man whom I chauffeured during my sophomore year, the year I wrote the original ten Paradoxical Commandments. That story is in the first book, as well. He couldn't climb stairs, and couldn't keep his food down, and was almost always irritable—but I learned how to help him, and it gave me a sense of meaning.

So how did I write the Paradoxical Commandments at age nineteen? I had learned from my parents, and I had learned from living in different states, attending different schools, studying world religions, being picketed, being run out of town, and chauffeuring an irascible old man who really didn't mean to be so irascible.

However, if there was one single experience behind the Paradoxical Commandments, it was the insight I had as I walked into the stadium at Roosevelt High School for the student awards ceremony at the end of my senior year in 1966. I had always cherished awards. I had always been very competitive. I was not only student body president, I was also the founder and manager of the school bookstore, and ROTC Band Commander, and so forth. Awards had always meant a lot to me.

But that day, as I walked into the stadium for the awards ceremony, it occurred to me that I was so happy about what I had done that year, and I felt so good about what I had learned and whom I had helped, that I didn't need any awards. *I had already been rewarded*. I already had the sense of meaning and satisfaction that came from doing a good job. The meaning and satisfaction were mine, whether or not anybody gave me an award.

That realization was a major breakthrough for me. I felt completely liberated, and completely at peace. I knew that if I did what was right and good and true, my actions would have their own intrinsic value. I would always find meaning. I didn't have to have the fame and glory. That was a fundamental insight that contributed to my writing the original ten Paradoxical Commandments a year and a half later.

Do you have a favorite commandment?

Yes, I do. But it's changed. Back in the sixties, when I wrote the original ten Paradoxical Commandments, I was focused on social and political change. At the time, I felt closest to the two commandments that were about establishing new ideas—the sixth and seventh commandments. The sixth commandment is:

The biggest men and women with the biggest ideas can be shot down by the smallest men and women with the smallest minds. Think big anyway.

The seventh commandment is:

People favor underdogs but follow only top dogs. Fight for a few underdogs anyway.

I also felt close to the tenth commandment:

Give the world the best you have and you'll get kicked in the teeth. Give the world the best you have anyway.

But today, while all ten Paradoxical Commandments are still important to me, my favorite commandment is the first one:

People are illogical, unreasonable, and self-centered. Love them anyway.

This commandment is about seeing beyond the faults and foibles of individuals to the good that is in them. It's about linking up with that goodness and building relationships. It's about loving people even when they are difficult.

I have to admit that when I wrote this commandment at age nineteen, I was really thinking that *everybody else* was illogical, unreasonable, and self-centered. It came as a big shock to discover, later in life, that *I* could be that way sometimes. I am grateful when people are still able to love me when I am being illogical, unreasonable, or self-centered, and I want to love them when they are that way, too. I think we have a desperate need for this kind of unconditional love in our world today.

Where did the Paradoxical Commandments travel?

I don't think anybody knows. All I know is that they have

been found all over the world, and have probably been seen and used by millions of people.

For twenty-five years after I wrote the Paradoxical Commandments, I didn't know they were on the move. What I know now is that people were putting them on their walls and refrigerator doors and into their speeches and articles. They were being used by businessmen, religious leaders, government officials, military leaders, teachers, coaches, rock stars, and students—people of many backgrounds and ages and circumstances, in many countries and cultures.

From using search engines on the Internet, I have learned that the Paradoxical Commandments have been used by the Boy Scouts in Canada and the United States; Rotarians in Malaysia, Hong Kong, and Alabama; the Cambodian Free Speech Movement; and a student leadership conference in South Africa. They have been translated into Japanese and used in homilies by a Japanese Catholic priest in Tokyo. They were used by Karl Menninger in a speech at the United Nations in 1981. They were used by a president of Zimbabwe. They have been used by a homeless shelter in Philadelphia, a welfare agency in Texas, a Methodist church in Kansas, a family council in Ohio, and the Oklahoma Girls State program.

They have been used in countless graduation speeches and sermons. They have been in *Reader's Digest*, and Ann Landers's column. I have seen them on websites for Catholic parishes, Protestant churches, and Mormon Sunday school teachers. They have been read out loud in synagogues in New York and Honolulu. They can be found in books by John C. Maxwell (*Becoming a Person of Influence*) and Wayne Dyer (*There's a Spiritual Solution to Every Problem*). They have been published in a newsletter of the Gordon Institute at Tufts University and on a website listing quotes from the monthly Harvard Business School Management Update. They have been used by trainers and by professional speakers in countless personal motivation seminars and presentations.

The list goes on—there are hundreds of examples. Nearly every day, I come across another one, or people contact me to share a sighting of their own. It is exciting to see where the Paradoxical Commandments have been!

Is there more than one version of the Paradoxical Commandments?

Sometimes, people who passed the Paradoxical Commandments on to their friends changed a few words, or added a phrase, or dropped a few of the commandments, or changed the title, or formatted the Paradoxical Commandments as a poem. There are versions of the Paradoxical Commandments that are known as "Anyway," "The Final Analysis," and "The Ten Commandments of Leadership." What is really remarkable, however, is that after traveling around the world for more than thirty years, most of the versions are true to the original ten Paradoxical Commandments as I first wrote them.

Did you ever imagine that the Paradoxical Commandments would travel all over the world and be used by millions of people?

No, never. I wrote the commandments for high school student leaders in the sixties, and my only hope was that some of the students would benefit from my message. I never imagined it would go any further than that.

Why do you think the Paradoxical Commandments have traveled around the world?

To be honest, I don't know why. But based on conversations with people who have used them, I have come up with four reasons that I think are good guesses.

First, I think the Paradoxical Commandments have traveled because they are a call to meaning, a call to live a meaningful life regardless of the whims of fate and twists of fortune that affect each of us. People are hungry for meaning, and the Paradoxical Commandments are about finding meaning.

Second, the commandments are fundamental and cut across different ideologies, theologies, and philosophies. They are about the things that we human beings have in common, not the doctrines that divide us. They have been useful to people of many faiths as well as no faith.

Third, I think they have traveled because they are short, easy to read, easy to put on a wall or inside a notebook, and easy to send to a friend or post on a website. They can be used as a kind of checklist. I have received messages from people who have told me that they look at the Paradoxical Commandments every morning before going to work.

Finally, I think they have spread around the world because they aren't questions or issues—they are commandments. They aren't wishy-washy. They don't say: Think about the possibility of maybe considering doing something. No—they say, Do it! And no excuses—Do it anyway!

What is the connection with Mother Teresa?

The Paradoxical Commandments were found on the wall of Mother Teresa's children's home in Calcutta. That fact was reported in a book compiled by Lucinda Vardey, *Mother Teresa: A Simple Path*, which was published in 1995. As a result, some people have attributed the Paradoxical Commandments to Mother Teresa.

I found out about it in September 1997 at my Rotary Club meeting. We usually begin each meeting with a prayer or a thought for the day, and a fellow Rotarian of mine got up and noted that Mother Teresa had died, and said that, in her memory, he wanted to read a poem she had written that was titled "Anyway." I bowed my head in contemplation and was astonished to recognize what he read—it was eight of the original ten Paradoxical Commandments.

I went up after the meeting and asked him where he got the poem. He said it was in a book about Mother Teresa, but he couldn't remember the title. So the next night I went to a bookstore and started looking through the shelf of books about the life and works of Mother Teresa. I found it, on the last page before the appendices in *Mother Teresa: A Simple Path*. The Paradoxical Commandments had been reformatted to look like a poem, and they had been retitled "Anyway." There was no author listed, but at the bottom of the page, it said: "From a sign on the wall of Shishu Bhavan, the children's home in Calcutta."

Mother Teresa, or one of her coworkers, thought that the Paradoxical Commandments were important enough to put up on the wall at the children's home, to look at, day after day, as they ministered to the children. That really hit me. I wanted to laugh, and cry, and shout—I was getting chills up and down my spine. Perhaps it hit me hard because I had a lot of respect for Mother Teresa, and perhaps because I knew something about children's homes. Whatever the reason, it had a huge impact on me. That was when I decided to speak and write about the Paradoxical Commandments again, thirty years after I first wrote them.

Have you always tried to live the Paradoxical Commandments? If so, how have they affected your own life and career?

Yes, I have always tried to live them. They are based on values I learned from my parents and my church, and they are part of my core being.

In terms of my career, living the commandments has affected the jobs I have chosen. I have sought work that was meaningful to me because it allowed me to make a positive difference in the lives of others. I have focused primarily on creating new jobs, improving educational opportunities, and strengthening services for children and families. I have taken on jobs that were "risky" in terms of traditional career paths because I was focused on meaning instead of power, pay, or prestige. I found that the risks were worth it because the meaning was always there.

Who are the biggest influences in your life?

My parents, my wife, my relatives, and my mentors. My parents had a huge impact on me. They lived their values and provided a wonderful example of what it meant to work hard, live a principled life, and be a strong family. Their example was reinforced by my relatives, who lived the same way. My wife has taught me about love and how my behavior impacts the people I love. I have had many mentors along the way—teachers and friends who stepped forward to give me their help and advice and point me in new directions. I have been extremely fortunate. Many people have loved and helped me. I am grateful to them, and I want to thank them by doing the same for others.

What books have had the biggest influence on your writing and thinking?

The first books that I can remember really having an impact on me were John F. Kennedy's *Profiles in Courage*, which I read in the seventh grade, and Henry David Thoreau's *Walden*, which I read in the ninth grade. My interest in personal meaning was heightened by reading Viktor Frankl's book, *Man's Search for Meaning*, in my first year or two of college, sometime around 1967. During the next twenty years, I was most influenced by the New International Version of the Bible and the writings of C. S. Lewis, especially *Mere Christianity*. In 1988, I read the first chapter of Robert Greenleaf's book, *Servant Leadership*, and I have been speaking and writing about servant leadership ever since.

While each of these books has had an important impact on me, the simple truth is that I love to read, and I have been influenced by hundreds of books.

What role do you see for the Paradoxical Commandments in our society in the future?

I hope that the Paradoxical Commandments will continue to

guide and inspire people to find personal meaning and deep happiness. The Paradoxical Commandments focus on the things that have given people personal meaning for centuries—loving people, helping people, and doing what is right and good and true. Personal meaning and deep happiness are available to each of us if we live the Paradoxical Commandments.

I wrote *Anyway: The Paradoxical Commandments* before the terrorist attack on September 11, 2001. That was a terrible tragedy. However, the way people responded, the way people pitched in and donated time and money, was inspiring. It has also been inspiring to see how many of us have sat down, reflected, refocused, and rededicated ourselves to the people and values that mean the most to us in our lives.

I think we need a sustained period of national rededication and renewal. We *know* what is most meaningful to us—family, friends, giving and receiving love. We know how to live. We just need the courage to live that way. If we remind ourselves, and encourage each other, we can *do it anyway.*

Acknowledgments

*I*n many ways, I wrote this book with my friends. I asked many friends, old and new, to share stories from their own lives. I also asked friends to comment on the draft of the book that emerged. My heartfelt thanks go to Wally Amos, Don Asman, Judy Asman, Magda Brisson, David Coleman, David Earles, Jerry Glashagel, Stu Gothold, Linda Serra Hagedorn, Will Hartzell, Ken Hill, John Howell, Jasmin Iwasaki, Wally Johnston, Paul Katz, Elizabeth Keith, Greg Kemp, Ed Kormondy, Wilson Lau, Scott Lewis, Norris Lineweaver, Les Miyamoto, Fran Newman, Hugh F. O'Reilly, Penny Patton, Mona Radice, Joe Rice, Sharon Royers, Jean Varney, Barbara Waugh, Steve Weiner, John Welshons, Jana Wolff, Vernon Wong, and Takeshi Yoshihara.

I am grateful to John Elder, publisher, and the entire team at Inner Ocean Publishing for their professionalism, enthusiasm, commitment, and friendship. I have enjoyed working very closely with Roger Jellinek, Senior Editor; Candida Tapia, Managing Editor, and Kirsten Whatley and Martha Cameron, copy editors. My thanks to Bill Greaves, art director, for his astonishing creativity, and to Marcy Goot, Ellen Peterson, Chana Clark, and Katie McMillan for their daily cooperation in marketing and public relations.

This book would not have been possible without the love and support of my wife, Elizabeth, who provided stories and ideas, and managed the family schedule to create time for me to write. I also want to thank Don Anderson and my colleagues at the YMCA of Honolulu for their understanding and cooperation during the times that I am traveling and speaking to share the Paradoxical Commandments.

About the Author

Dr. Kent M. Keith was raised in six states. He has been an attorney, a state government official, a high-tech park developer, president of a private university, a graduate school lecturer, and a community organizer. He is currently senior vice president of the YMCA of Honolulu. He earned his B.A. from Harvard University, his M.A. from Oxford University, his certificate in Japanese from Waseda University, his law degree from the University of Hawai'i, and his doctorate in education from the University of Southern California.

Dr. Keith has given and presented hundreds of speeches and conference papers on law, ocean technology, energy, economic development, secondary school activities, education, management, servant leadership, and the needs of youth. He is a Rhodes Scholar. In 1984 he was chosen as one of the Ten Outstanding Young Men of America by the United States Jaycees. In 1993 he was a University of Hawai'i Distinguished Alumni awardee.

Dr. Keith is known nationally and internationally as the author of the Paradoxical Commandments, which he wrote and published in 1968 at the age of nineteen. The first edition of his book *The Paradoxical Commandments: Finding Personal Meaning in a Crazy World* was published by Inner Ocean Publishing of Maui in October 2001. A new edition, titled *Anyway: The Paradoxical Commandments*, was published by G. P. Putnam's Sons in April 2002, and has become a national bestseller. The rights to his book have been sold in twenty countries.

Dr. Keith has appeared on the front page of *The New York Times* and has been featured in *People* magazine, *The Washington Post*, *The San Francisco Chronicle*, and *Family Circle*. He was interviewed by Katie Couric on NBC's "Today Show," and has appeared on a dozen TV shows and more than seventy radio programs in the United States, the United Kingdom, and Australia.

Dr. Keith lives in Manoa Valley, Honolulu, with his wife, Elizabeth, and their three children, Kristina, Spencer, and Angela. He is available for speaking engagements. He can be contacted through www.paradoxicalcommandments.com.

Inner Ocean Publishing

*Expanding horizons
with books that
challenge the mind,
inspire the spirit,
and nourish the soul.*

We invite you to visit us at:
www.innerocean.com

Inner Ocean Publishing, Inc.
PO Box 1239, Makawao
Maui, HI 96768, USA
Email: info@innerocean.com